Friedrich Hölderlin

Twayne's World Authors Series

German Literature

Ulrich Weisstein, Editor
Indiana University

TWAS 738

Friedrich Hölderlin

By Richard Unger

University of Georgia

Twayne Publishers • *Boston*

Friedrich Hölderlin

Richard Unger

Copyright © 1984 by G. K. Hall & Company
All Rights Reserved
Published by Twayne Publishers
A Division of G. K. Hall & Company
70 Lincoln Street
Boston, Massachusetts 02111

Book Production by Marne B. Sultz

Book Design by Barbara Anderson

Printed on permanent/durable acid-free
paper and bound in the United States of
America.

**Library of Congress Cataloging in
Publication Data**

Unger, Richard, 1939–
Friedrich Hölderlin.

(Twayne's world authors series; TWAS
738. German literature)
Bibliography: p. 147
Includes index.
1. Hölderlin, Friedrich, 1770–1843—
Criticism and interpretation. I. Title.
II. Series: Twayne's world
authors series ; TWAS 738.
III. Series: Twayne's world
authors series. German literature.
PT2359.H2U44   1984   831'.6
83-26582
ISBN 0-8057-6585-9

Contents

About the Author

Professor Unger was born in 1939 in Springfield, Illinois. He received the A.B. in 1961 from St. Louis University, the M.A. in 1962 from Cornell University, and the Ph.D. in 1967 also from Cornell. He has taught at the University of Missouri-St. Louis, Emory University, and Mississippi State University, and is presently associate professor of comparative literature at the University of Georgia. His publications include *Hölderlin's Major Poetry: The Dialectics of Unity,* an essay on Hölderlin in the forthcoming *European Writers: The Romantic Century,* and articles on various comparative literature topics.

Preface

Among educated Germans today Hölderlin is generally regarded as one of Germany's two or three greatest poets. For various reasons, however, his poetry is not widely known among American readers. Perhaps the principal reason is the extreme difficulty of his best work. Because of their syntactical and intellectual complexity, his poems are (even for Germans) very hard to read in the original, and even the best translations often fail to convey the full meaning and esthetic quality of the original poetry. Thus, despite his extremely high status in German-speaking lands throughout most of this century, Hölderlin's work has never been as *exportable* as the more accessible poetry of Goethe, Heine, or Rilke.

It is precisely the intellectual density and complexity of Hölderlin's writings that should make one question whether it is possible to offer an even marginally adequate account of his work in a book of this size and format. Thus, for example, anyone familiar with Hölderlin scholarship would consider it foolhardy to attempt, in such a limited number of pages, complete interpretations of hymns such as "Der Rhein," "Friedensfeier," and "Patmos." And, of course, I am making no such attempts in this book. Rather, in most cases, I am offering (admittedly inadequate) paraphrastic summaries of Hölderlin's works together with indications of what I think they might mean. This procedure is intended only to provide assistance to readers encountering the poet for the first time. Those seeking understanding of the texts beyond the most elementary level are referred to the voluminous critical literature partially listed in the notes and bibliography.

In my discussions of many of Hölderlin's poems, I am, of course, indebted to a great many previous studies of Hölderlin, but most especially to the information and analyses offered by Friedrich Beissner and Jochen Schmidt in the notes to the two-volume Insel edition.[1] Beissner and Adolf Beck were editors of the standard *Grosse Stuttgarter Ausgabe* of the poet's works.[2] Schmidt, in his many books and articles, has consistently distinguished himself by his exact and detailed elucidations of Hölderlin's texts. His analyses are thus perhaps the most immediately useful of the many excellent studies of Hölderlin that have appeared in the last several decades. My footnotes bear witness to my heavy indebtedness to his work, as well as to studies by other prominent scholars, such as Beissner, Beck, Wolfgang Binder, Peter Szondi, and Lawrence Ryan.

The present book begins with an introductory chapter on Hölderlin's life and then proceeds to consider his early writings in a roughly chronological order. Chapter 2, "Early Poetry," covers verse written before ca. 1798, while the *"Hyperion"* chapter deals with the novel Hölderlin completed during the latter part of the same period. "Der Tod des Empedokles" was the fragmentary play Hölderlin worked on chiefly during 1798–99. Chapters 5 through 8, dealing with the later poetry, are arranged according to genre, chapter 5 covering the odes, 6 the elegies, and 7 and 8 Hölderlin's most important productions, the Pindaric hymns. The final chapter offers a brief account of German readers' responses to the poet during the last two centuries. All quotations of Hölderlin's work are from the *Grosse Stuttgarter Ausgabe,* although the archaic original spelling has been modernized. The translations (which are intended to be as literal as possible) are in all cases my own; some of them have appeared in my earlier book on Hölderlin.[3]

Finally, I would like to express my gratitude toward those who have been of greatest assistance during the years I have been working on this book: Maria Kohler, who has been of great help to me during my many visits to the Hölderlin-Archiv in Stuttgart; Professor Ulrich Weisstein, without whose patience and support this project could not have been brought to completion; Lynn Whittaker, who was of considerable help in enabling me to revise many chapters; and my many forbearing and diligent typists. I would also like to thank the American Philosophical Society for a grant that enabled me to work in Stuttgart one summer, and the Comparative Literature Department of the University of Georgia, which has been unstinting in providing me with the indispensable money for summer research.

Richard Unger

University of Georgia

Chronology

1770   March 20, Johann Christian Friedrich Hölderlin born in Lauffen am Neckar, Württemberg; eldest child of Heinrich Friedrich Hölderlin, custodian of former monastic estates, and Johanna Christiana Heyn.

1772   July 5, father dies at age thirty-six.

1774   October 10, mother marries Johann Christoph Gock. Family moves to Nürtingen, Württemberg.

1779   March 13, stepfather dies.

1776–1783   Attends school in Nürtingen.

1784   Enters Cloister-School at Denkendorf near Nürtingen. Composes earliest verses.

1786   Graduates to Higher Cloister-School at Maulbronn.

1788–1793   Attends Lutheran Seminary (*Stift*) at Tübingen. Friendship with fellow-seminarians Hegel and Schelling. Poems first published in G. H. Stäudlin's *Musenalmanach fürs Jahr 1792*. Begins work on novel, *Hyperion*.

1793   After graduating from seminary in September, assumes position of private tutor with the family of Charlotte von Kalb in Waltershausen, Saxony (December 28).

1794   In Waltershausen, works on early drafts of *Hyperion*.

1795   Dismissed from von Kalb household in January. Goes to Jena, attends lectures by Fichte; contact with Schiller and Goethe; friendship with Isaac von Sinclair. May or June, abruptly leaves Jena and returns to mother's house in Nürtingen.

1796   Enters employment as tutor at house of banker Jacob Gontard in Frankfurt am Main; falls in love with Jacob's wife Susette ("Diotima").

1797   Happily in love with Susette; first volume of *Hyperion* published. Works on Empedocles drama.

1798   After an altercation with Jacob, resigns position with Gontard family in September. At Sinclair's urging, goes to Homburg, where Sinclair is active at the court of the Landgraf. Clandestine visits with Susette later in year.

1799   In Homburg, works on Empedocles dramas. Second volume of *Hyperion* published (October).

1800   Last meeting with Susette in May. Returns to Nürtingen in June; later goes to stay with merchant Christian Landauer in Stuttgart. Writes elegies, including "Brot und Wein."

1801   Assumes third tutorial position with Gonzenbach family in Hauptwil, Switzerland; politely dismissed from it and returns to Nürtingen (April). Writes "Heimkunft," "Der Rhein," and several major odes, including "Dichterberuf."

1802   Fourth and last tutorial position, with family of consul D. C. Meyer in Bordeaux. Resigns in May and, after wandering through France, arrives in Nürtingen in a state of evident insanity. Susette Gontard dies June 22. In calmer intervals, Hölderlin works on poetry.

1803   January 30, "Patmos" presented to the Landgraf of Homburg. Hölderlin remains in Nürtingen, works on translations of Sophocles and Pindar.

1804   Publishes translations of *Oedipus Rex* and *Antigone*. Sinclair brings him to Homburg, where he is given sinecure of "court librarian."

1805   Sinclair tried for high treason in Württemberg. In Homburg, Hölderlin's psychic condition worsens considerably.

1806   Forcibly transported from Homburg to a clinic in Tübingen (September).

1807   Entrusted to care of Tübingen carpenter Ernst Zimmer; quartered in tower adjoining house.

1807–1843   Remains with Zimmer family; never recovers sanity. After Zimmer's death in 1838, cared for by Zimmer's daughter Lotte.

1815   April 29, death of Sinclair.

1826   Publication of first collected edition of Hölderlin's poetry, edited by G. Schwab and L. Uhland.

1828   February 17, death of Hölderlin's mother.

1831   Publication of Wilhelm Waiblinger's *Friedrich Hölderlins Leben, Dichtung, and Wahnsinn.* (Waiblinger, a young student, had been a frequent visitor and companion of the poet during the 1820s.)

1843   June 7, death of Hölderlin at age 73.

Chapter One
Hölderlin in Context

Johann Christian Friedrich Hölderlin was born of a middle-class family in the small town of Lauffen on the Neckar in the Swabian duchy of Württemberg on March 20, 1770—the birth year also of Beethoven, Hegel and Wordsworth.[1] His father, Heinrich Friedrich Hölderlin, an overseer of former monastic estates, died in 1772, and in 1774 his mother married Johann Christoph Gock, an old friend of her husband. The family then moved to Nürtingen. When his stepfather died in 1779, Friedrich was deeply affected both by the event and by the serious religious depression to which his mother then succumbed.

An important psychological analysis of the poet and his work contends that the lack of a father was to have a decisive influence on him throughout his life.[2] It could be argued, too, that the general atmosphere of gloom about his maternal home might be responsible, in part, for the intense seriousness of his poetic work. Another influence was that of Pietism, a movement within the Lutheran Church that stressed intense emotional subjectivity in religious devotion. Critics have noted that Pietistic habits of thought and feeling contributed to the introverted emotionalism of much of Hölderlin's early work; and that certain Pietistic writings had some influence on the ideas expressed in some of his later hymns.[3] It seems that young Friedrich, embued with such seriousness, did not associate very much with other children but instead developed an almost Wordsworthian rapport with the countryside surrounding Nürtingen.

Friedrich completed his primary schooling at Nürtingen with emphasis on religion and the dead languages, for his devout mother had decided that he was to be a minister in the state-supported Lutheran Church. In 1784, at the age of fourteen, he entered the Cloister School at nearby Denkendorf to commence the first phase of training. The place was, as the name implies, a former monastery and, though Protestant, was dominated by a virtually monastic spirit of ascetic discipline; Hölderlin hated it.[4] In October 1786, he was transferred to the Higher Cloister School at Maulbronn. The discipline there was less rigorous than that at Denkendorf but the course of studies was still uninspiring. However, his enthusiastic temperament found expression in a number of intense friendships and also in his first love affair, with Louise Nast, the daughter of a school official. In autumn, 1788, he graduated from Maulbronn to the Lutheran Seminary (or *Stift*) at Tübingen.

The Tübingen Stift had long been considered the intellectual center of Württemberg; it produced among the droves of dutiful servants of the church such radically heterodox thinkers as Friedrich Hegel, Friedrich Wilhelm Schelling, and Hölderlin himself.[5] All three men attended the seminary at a time when the institution was in a period of relative decline. Hölderlin immediately established himself as a good student but succumbed quickly to the prevailing mood of disgruntlement over the depressing atmosphere of the place. Yet here, again, he formed intense friendships with those who could share not only his discontent but also his enthusiasm for poetry.

During Hölderlin's second year at the Stift, Karl Eugen, duke of Württemberg, paid an official visit to the institution, ordered the administration to devise a more rigorous set of rules, publicly interrogated the assembled seminarians concerning their belief in God, and decreed that the director should report to him all students who had violated any regulations. Hölderlin's outrage at these developments exacerbated the contempt he already felt for the institution.[6] His indignation found an outlet in a growing interest in and enthusiasm for the intellectual and political ideals of the French Revolution. Such ideals were expressed in the poetry he wrote at the time, particularly the series, "Hymns to the Ideals of Mankind," strongly influenced by the thought and poetry of Schiller.

Other enthusiasms were also awakening. He fell in love again, this time with Elise Lebret, the daughter of the school chancellor. He managed to publish a few of his recent poems. Most significantly, perhaps, he was assigned to share a dormitory room with Schelling and Hegel, under whose influence he began the study of Kantian metaphysics. The roommates also read Leibnitz, Plato, and Rousseau, as well as Friedrich Heinrich Jacobi, whose essay on Spinoza had unleashed a spirited debate among German intellectuals on the topic of pantheism vis-à-vis Christian dogma.[7] Hölderlin's increased interest in political topics was further enhanced during 1792 by events both at the Stift and in the outside world. In February, the duke proclaimed his new set of rules, which most students considered overly severe; 1792 also saw the beginning of the first coalition wars against France. The seminarians viewed France's enemies,

Prussia and Austria, as larger embodiments of the same spirit of German despotism exemplified in the policies of the duke. Thus, many sided enthusiastically with the French against the German autocracies. About this time, Hölderlin decided to make political engagement the central theme of a novel.

Hölderlin's last year at the Stift was marked by an intensification of his loneliness, while he worked on poems and on his novel, *Hyperion*; continued to study Kant, Plato, and Greek literature; and worried about what to do after graduation—for he was now resolved not to become a clergyman. A break came when a friend recommended him to Schiller (already one of his literary heroes), who was seeking to find a tutor for the son of his friend Charlotte von Kalb, in Walterhausen, Saxony. In the fall, soon after graduation, Hölderlin had an interview with Schiller, who was favorably impressed by him and recommended him for the position. After returning to his mother's house in Nürtingen for several weeks, Hölderlin set out for Walterhausen and arrived at the von Kalb residence on December 28, 1793.

His position as educator of the nine-year-old Fritz von Kalb was the first of Hölderlin's four tutorial jobs; in this, as in the others, he failed to meet the expectations of his employers and was forced to leave under distressing circumstances. Although different factors were at work in each case, Hölderlin inevitably began each job with great optimism, even euphoria, and ended it in disappointment. In each case he departed with warm letters of recommendation, all commending the nobility of his character. But each time, there seemed to be compelling reasons for his dismissal.[8]

His employment with the von Kalbs set the pattern. During the first months of 1794 he was elated with his situation at the aristocratic house, and his letters spoke of how well he was treated. Hölderlin soon had to observe, however, that his pupil was frequently sullen, rude, and intractable. Eventually, Herr von Kalb informed the tutor that his son was afflicted with a "certain vice," which was then assumed to cause mental and physical degeneration and make its victims nasty and unteachable. He urged Hölderlin to do whatever he could to keep young Fritz from masturbating. Hölderlin, disgusted and horrified, solemnly undertook to rescue the boy from his nefarious practices, becoming at first merely watchful, but eventually having to sit all night at the boy's bedside in unremitting vigilance. Hölderlin thus was often tired and irritable; he began to show impatience in his regular tutorial activities and to conduct himself unsociably toward his employers, who were becoming dissatisfied with his work.

Hölderlin's constant vigil over Fritz also had the effect of depriving him of his philosophical and literary studies. Earlier in the year he had had time to work on his novel and to study Kant, Herder, and Fichte, whose *Wissenschaftslehre* had just appeared. He had also read Schiller's new essay, *Über Anmut und Würde,* and had maintained a sporadic correspondence with the author. But now he had no time for such activities. In November, the von Kalbs, who felt sorry for the overworked tutor, encouraged him and Fritz to visit Jena, then one of the intellectual centers of Germany. Hölderlin now had an opportunity to meet influential people and advance his career. He attended lectures by Fichte at the university and paid several visits to Schiller, once even encountering Goethe, on whom he made a rather unfavorable impression. Meanwhile, he became increasingly more impatient with his pupil's vileness and stupidity, so that finally he began venting his frustration by beating the child. In January 1795, Hölderlin was persuaded to resign his position, receiving three months' salary as severance pay.

The year 1795 was crucial in Hölderlin's life and brought to a kind of disastrous climax the early phase of his human and intellectual development.[9] His plan, after returning to Jena, was to live as frugally as possible. He hoped to formulate a philosophical position that would synthesize Kantian esthetic and ethical theories with the principles of Platonic idealism. He also hoped to complete his novel, a fragmentary early version of which had already been published in October 1794 in Schiller's periodical, *Die neue Thalia.* Schiller offered to let Hölderlin collaborate in his forthcoming publication, *Die Horen,* and found Hölderlin a prospective publisher who gave him a small payment in advance for his novel. Nevertheless, however, Hölderlin was living in penury and eating only one meal a day. His physical and mental health, already weakened, began to deteriorate; he was now suffering from periods of profound depression. He soon withdrew from society and was seeing virtually no one except Fichte and Schiller. Then, however, he befriended a law student whom he had already met briefly in Tübingen, the nineteen-year-old Isaac von Sinclair, who had important connections at the court of Homburg-Hessen.[10] Sinclair was then a fiery adherent of the most radically democratic ideals, and he may have succeeded in reviving some of Hölderlin's political enthusiasms. About the beginning of June, however, Hölderlin suddenly and without warning left Jena and returned to Nürtingen. This abrupt departure apparently surprised several people and offended Schiller, who expected him to continue work on *Die Horen.* No satisfactory reason has ever been adduced for this erratic and irresponsible act.[11]

On his way home, Hölderlin heard that a wealthy family in Frankfurt were looking for a tutor for their son. Despite his disillusionment with tutoring, he needed some kind of employment at this time. (He had signed an agreement at the beginning of his seminary training, stating that once his education was completed he would serve the Württemberg state church wherever and in whatever capacity its administrative board should choose. But the board also had the option of granting occupational deferments to theologians who had accepted some respectable temporary job.) First, however, he needed some time to recuperate at his mother's house in Nürtingen. Hölderlin's depression was intense and prolonged because of the recent failure of his ambitions to become a successful writer.[12] His intellectual world was also in a shambles, for his earlier belief in the pantheistic unity of man, God, and nature had been shattered by the study of the writings of Kant and Fichte, which insisted upon the radical alienation of man from nature and divine life. One motive for his intense philosophical studies of the past year had been to discover a monistic position that would withstand criticism; there, too, he had failed.

The offer of the tutorial position finally came through in December 1795. Hölderlin accepted immediately and in January 1796 began his duties as tutor for the eight-year-old Henry Gontard. Henry's father, Jakob Gontard, was a prominent and highly successful banker and businessman in Frankfurt. His wife, Susette, was a beautiful, cultured and sensitive young woman, one year older than Hölderlin. Hölderlin fell in love with her almost immediately. She returned his affection and quickly became the focal point of his entire emotional, spiritual, and metaphysical universe.

Hölderlin's biographer Wilhelm Michel has given us an interesting interpretation of their relationship, based on their letters and on Hölderlin's treatment of "Diotima" in his literary works.[13] Michel points out that Hölderlin had already depicted, in the character of Melite in the earlier versions of *Hyperion,* a female ideal of human perfection, modeled closely after the concept of the "Schöne Seele" as expounded especially in Schiller's *Über Anmut und Würde.* Briefly, the "beautiful soul" is one in which "reason" and "the senses" are perfectly harmonized, so that one is naturally good and acts according to the highest principles of (Kantian) morality quite spontaneously and unreflectively. This was the highly idealized moral stereotype with which Hölderlin soon came to associate—and identify—the real Susette Gontard. The heroine of his novel was renamed Diotima, after the wise woman in Plato's *Symposium* who instructed Socrates in the mysteries of supernal eros, and made to conform to the personality of the Diotima who was Hölderlin's idealized version of Susette. And, just as for Hyperion in the novel, this Diotima was apparently for Hölderlin himself a means of spiritual salvation. Like Socrates' Diotima, she made real for him the essences of cosmic love and supernal beauty; she also, in Hölderlin's view, became a living example of the reconciliation of spirit and nature, which Hölderlin had vainly attempted to reconcile conceptually within the framework of Kantian and Fichtean metaphysics. Intellectually, he was now able, by direct personal intuition, to resolve the problem of the mind's alienation from the natural world. And, personally, he felt that, by beholding, loving, and ultimately participating in Diotima's divine beauty of soul, he himself was able to attain a wholeness, harmony, and radiance of unified being which he had never before experienced. Thus (as Michel observes) Hölderlin's relationship with Susette had, from his perspective, more the character of a Christ experience than that of a petty employee's affair with the boss's wife.

The first volume of *Hyperion* was published in April 1797, and Hölderlin sent a copy to Schiller, along with two of his most recent poems, "An den Aether" and "Der Wanderer," which Schiller agreed to publish. The relationship between Hölderlin and Susette, however, which had gone smoothly during 1796 and the first half of 1797, was now threatened with disruption. Herr Gontard, although aware of the situation, had not been unduly jealous, for he had seemed to view the relationship as purely spiritual; yet he was becoming increasingly irritated at Hölderlin's arrogance and airs of superiority. The tutor had in effect assumed spiritual leadership of the household and made an ardent devotee of his wife. Thus by midsummer 1797, Gontard had apparently decided to relegate the tutor to his proper place. Hölderlin, always extremely sensitive to any abuse, was outraged at this affront to his dignity. The situation came to its disastrous resolution in September 1798. It is probable that Gontard finally lost all patience at Hölderlin's attentions to his wife and roundly told him off.[14] This drastic humiliation was intolerable to the poet, who immediately left the house in a rage. He moved to nearby Homburg, where his friend Sinclair greeted him warmly, gave him all possible comfort, and found him a place to stay. Sinclair also sought to get Hölderlin involved in the social and intellectual life of the Landgraf's court. Yet Hölderlin was disconsolate over his separation from Susette.

They managed to exchange letters; all of Susette's have been preserved, but only four of Hölderlin's. The letters tend to confirm that the lovers actually regarded their relationship as idealistically as did Hyperion and Diotima in the novel. Beginning in the fall of that year, they managed to arrange a number of secret meetings.

For the most part, Hölderlin used the enforced leisure of his stay in Homburg to rethink the basic premises of his attitude toward poetry and the relationship between poetry and life. In October, he wrote his mother that he wanted to spend a year in total dedication to his poetic work in yet another attempt to establish himself as a successful writer. He was now working on the early drafts of an intended classical tragedy based on the life of Empedocles. He had become interested in the life and teachings of that pre-Socratic philosopher and had decided to write a play concentrating both on the social conflicts in Empedocles' world and on his religiously motivated suicide. Hölderlin's renewed interest in social issues was stimulated by contacts with the radical democrats who were Sinclair's friends at the Homburg court. Also, probably to distract Hölderlin from his romantic agonies, Sinclair had encouraged him to attend as a visitor the Rastatt Congress, where Sinclair (though only twenty-two) was the official representative of the Landgraf. Hölderlin, however, continued to correspond with Susette, sometimes resorting to exchanging letters with her through a hedge. He was, moreover, able to visit her a few times in Frankfurt and elsewhere.

Hölderlin's chief professional venture in 1799 was his attempt to found and edit a literary periodical named *Iduna,* a "journal of esthetic content for ladies."[15] The project failed to gain adequate support, and Hölderlin was once again discouraged and embittered. He was also again out of money, and it was always humiliating for him to ask his mother for continuing financial support.

The second volume of *Hyperion* appeared in October, and Hölderlin dedicated his first copy to Susette Gontard. He continued his attempts to mold his Empedocles material into an authentic Greek tragedy, although he was soon forced to abandon it. Connected with his efforts on the play were a number of abstruse theoretical essays written at this time. Some, such as "Das Werden im Vergehen," were mainly concerned with patterns of historical development; others, such as "Wechsel der Töne" and "Über die Verfahrungsweise des poetischen Geistes," were addressed to problems of poetic form and composition.[16] His poetic productions, aside from a few experiments in the elegiac form, were chiefly Alcaic odes, some of them developed from epigrammatic verses composed earlier. Engaged in these projects, but becoming progressively more depressed over his situation, he remained in Homburg throughout 1799.

Hölderlin remained in a state of depression throughout the early months of 1800. Despite the attempts of his Homburg friends to cheer him up, his gloom continued to deepen, partly because of his awareness that he and Susette could never be together again and partly because of his generally worsening mental condition. Also, he felt that he needed to be alone more in order to devote time to his poetic endeavors. He had a strong, unexplainable urge to move out of his present situation. In March, at the death of his brother-in-law, his mother urged him to come home to help comfort his bereaved sister. In early May, Hölderlin had a last clandestine meeting with Susette, and in June, despite the urgings of his friends, he returned home to Nürtingen, remaining there only a few weeks. He then traveled to Stuttgart for a protracted stay with his friend Christian Landauer, a wealthy and well-educated merchant.

The summer and fall of 1800 was for Hölderlin a time of relative peace and contentment.[17] Moreover, in a highly congenial atmosphere, his poetic output became astoundingly copious and brilliant. He succeeded in composing a number of poems far better than anything he had previously written, such as the elegies "Menons Klagen um Diotima" and "Brot und Wein" and the ode "Natur und Kunst oder Saturn und Jupiter." In the two elegies he developed a philosophy of history: that the divine presence that had been known and celebrated by the Greeks and had disappeared with the end of Hellenic civilization would become manifest to men again in contemporary Europe, and that poets (particularly German poets such as himself) were to be the prophets and priests of this new universal epiphany. With this divine calling in mind, he was becoming ever more fervently convinced of the sacredness of his poetic concerns.

While in Stuttgart, he at first endeavored to support himself by giving private lessons in philosophy, but he soon found the income insufficient and felt impelled once again to seek a full-time tutorial position. When such a position was offered to him by the von Gonzenbach family in Hauptwil, Switzerland, he accepted it. He departed for Hauptwil and arrived there in January 1801.

His duty there, once again, was to educate the young children—in this case, two girls—of a wealthy businessman. Once again he at first found his employers most pleasant and his duties most congenial. Moreover, he was for a while elated at the prospect of imminent peace in Europe, a peace that was soon to be established by the Treaty of Lunéville in February 1801.[18]

Although it was to prove only an interlude in the Napoleonic wars, Hölderlin was then convinced that it was the herald of a forthcoming golden age which would see the establishment of "the holy supremacy of love and goodness" and the unification of all men in a holy "communal spirit." The Germans, especially, would profit from this new condition, which would foster an unfolding of the secret inner forces within their souls. (These sentiments would eventually find their fruition in the great hymn "Friedensfeier.") Hölderlin was also elated by his proximity to the Alps, which appeared to him a "marvelous legend from the heroic youth of our Mother Earth." His religious response to the Alps, as well as his fresh millennial expectations, would find expression in such poems as "Der Rhein" and the elegy "Heimkunft."

The homecoming described in the elegy took place in April. Although Hölderlin had every reason to be happy and successful in his work, the gradual deterioration of his mental condition, which his friends had been observing since 1798, was probably apparent also to his new employers. His moods and behavior probably seemed sufficiently strange to them to discourage their permitting him to continue in charge of their children. He was thus relieved of his duties under a polite but transparent pretext. Hölderlin seemed to feel no bitterness on this occasion; perhaps his sense of growing intimacy with nature and the gods had by now precluded mundane resentments. His April homecoming, as recounted in "Heimkunft," seems to have been one of holy expectation and joy.

Once at home, however, his initial euphoria abated and he had again to contend with his loving but exasperated mother and with the Württemberg church, which was threatening to draft him into parish service. He wrote a final letter to Schiller, asking for help in securing a lectureship in Greek literature at Jena.[19] Like a previous letter, this one remained unanswered. Schiller had by now written him off forever as a hopeless eccentric. Hölderlin could not hope to support himself by writing and selling poetry, although by August he had managed to negotiate the publication of several recent poems. In autumn he was once again compelled to accept the offer of a tutorial position, this time with Daniel Christoph Meyer, a German consul in Bordeaux, France.

In letters written in December 1801, Hölderlin expressed his mixed feelings on once again leaving his fatherland.[20] Although thoroughly "German" at heart and totally dedicated to his compatriots, he felt that he needed to get away to gain greater clarity regarding their holy destiny. In a very important letter of December 4 to his friend Casimir Böhlendorff, he expatiates on the essential differences between ancient Greek and modern

Western art. He distinguishes between the "fire from heaven" which was natural to the Greeks and the "clarity of representation" which is native to ourselves. Just as the Greeks needed to learn clarity (as in their classical art) in order to achieve formal articulation of their fiery impulses, so we must appropriate for ourselves some of the burning inspiration that was innate to the Greeks but originally alien to us. For us, too, a synthesis between intensity and clarity is needed. Yet our synthesis must necessarily take a different form than that achieved by the Greeks. Hence, Hölderlin felt, neoclassical insistence on imitating the *forms* of Greek art has been basically mistaken. We should rather emulate the artistic *intensity* of the Greeks; once such intensity is acquired we might succeed in that which (although innate) is paradoxically most difficult for us, the development of our own, properly Western mode of formal clarity and perfection.

When Hölderlin arrived in Bordeaux in January 1802, he was warmly greeted by the Meyer family. They assured him that he would be happy there, and, as in all previous cases, he believed them. But once again the pattern was fulfilled. His first letters home were joyous and optimistic. Then his correspondence became less frequent and showed increasing disturbance of mind and spirit. In May, his employment was discontinued, perhaps in recognition of his virtual insanity. The circumstances surrounding his departure are unclear, but, as always, the letter of recommendation was wholly laudatory.[21] After leaving Bordeaux, Hölderlin took the road to Paris. Later correspondence and some of his later poetry preserve a number of his impressions of the region around Bordeaux and the areas traversed on his return journey through France. Most significantly, he tells of the "fire of Heaven," the intense sunlight now clearly mythologized as a divine presence overwhelming his senses. In a later letter, he remarks that "as one might say of heroes . . . Apollo has struck me."[22]

His condition became clear to everyone after his return to Swabia in late June. He first visited Stuttgart, where his friends immediately recognized his insanity. One describes him as "pale as a corpse, emaciated, with wild, hollow eyes, long hair and beard, and clothed like a beggar."[23] He went home to Nürtingen, where his family were equally horrified at his mental and physical condition. He returned to Stuttgart; his condition began to improve somewhat, but then in early July, he received a letter from Sinclair stating that Susette Gontard had died of a contagious disease on June 22.[24] This news seems to have destroyed whatever remained of Hölderlin's mental balance. He fled to Nürtingen, where he was put under the care of a physician. By then, he was suffering from fits of violent rage, which could only be calmed if someone read aloud to him from Homer. He remained at home in this condition until the end of September.

That fall, Sinclair, who had been urging Hölderlin to visit him in Homburg, decided to invite him to come with him to the Congress of Regensburg, a peace conference at which Sinclair was acting as ambassador. Sinclair hoped that the distraction would have a good effect on him, and indeed, his condition seemed to improve there. Before Hölderlin left for home, Sinclair may have informed him of the Landgraf's desire that Hölderlin write a religious poem contemplating the present historical moment from a Christian perspective. Hölderlin's response was the impressive (if unorthodox) hymn "Patmos," which he composed that winter and presented to the Landgraf in January 1803. Hölderlin's other major poetic productions of this period (their exact dating is not possible) include the last of his completed hymns: "Der Einzige," "Der Ister," "Andenken," and "Mnemosyne." His most significant letter of that year was written to Böhlendorff in November.[25] It continued, in a less coherent fashion than the previous letter, his meditations on the essential differences between Greek and modern art and civilization. He asserts that modern German poets are now beginning for the first time "since the Greeks . . . to sing in a properly native [*vaterländisch*] and natural, actually original" fashion.[26] The modern poets, now fully schooled in the alien intensity of Greek art, are discovering their own proper mode of "clarity of representation" mentioned in the earlier letter.

Through much of 1803, Hölderlin appeared wholly immersed in literary work, which now largely consisted of translating Sophocles' *Oedipus Rex* and *Antigone,* a project begun several years earlier. He had found a publisher for these translations and even hoped that they might be performed at Weimar. It, of course, helped his condition somewhat that the translations had been found acceptable; some recent poems had likewise been accepted for publication.

In May 1804, Sinclair finally devised a pretext for getting Hölderlin to come to Homburg: he invented for him a fictitious job as court librarian to which he attached a real salary, which he himself would secretly pay. Hölderlin, who in his lucid phases wanted to retain some sense of dignity and social usefulness, accepted the offer, much to his mother's misgivings. In June, Sinclair came to Nürtingen to escort his friend to Homburg. Hölderlin went with him, not realizing that he would never see the town or his mother again. Hölderlin was warmly received by Sinclair's circle in Homburg and by the Landgraf, who had been favorably impressed with his poem "Patmos." He did no actual work in the court library, although he probably did some reading there. Sinclair at first tended to be skeptical about the extent of his friend's insanity, often suspecting that his confused and incoherent way of speaking was really a kind of ruse of deliberate eccentricity, "a mode of expression assumed for well-considered reasons."[27] For whatever reason, his stay in Homburg at first seemed beneficial for him.

Early in 1805, however, the tranquility of his life there was destroyed. Sinclair was accused of conspiracy to commit high treason against the prince of Württemberg.[28] (Sinclair had, in fact, while in Stuttgart the previous June, had some meetings with local radicals, among whom the possibility of revolution against the tyrannical prince was presumably discussed.) He was arrested, transported to Stuttgart, imprisoned, and put on trial. Unfortunately, Hölderlin was implicated in the procedure, and the shock of Sinclair's arrest and the charge of his own implication temporarily set him back into total, raving madness. Although Hölderlin's own extradition was also demanded, the Landgraf sought to avoid it. Hölderlin was officially examined by a doctor in Homburg, who sent to Stuttgart his testimony that Hölderlin was clinically insane. That seemed to satisfy the Württemberg authorities. In July the charges against Sinclair also were dropped, and he was released and permitted to return to Homburg.

There are few reports on Hölderlin's condition for about a year. It may be assumed, however, that there was a slow, gradual deterioration. In his better moments, he may have worked on translating the hymns of Pindar, a project he had recently undertaken; he may also have written some of the sketches of hymnic verse that have come to us as fragments. Then, in the summer of 1806, developments made it impossible for Sinclair to continue his support of Hölderlin in Homburg. Thus, Sinclair concluded, it was finally necessary that he be taken away. His mother concurred, and on September 11, 1806, Hölderlin was forcibly transported in a coach, despite his furious resistance, to Tübingen. There he was confined in a clinic, where he was often forced to wear a kind of straitjacket and a facial mask. After nearly a year in the clinic, Hölderlin's condition had worsened so that its director concluded that he was incurable. Thus when a local master carpenter and cabinetmaker, Ernst Zimmer, offered to care for Hölderlin in his own home, the director assented and the poet was moved to his new home in summer, 1807. Zimmer was an intelligent, well-to-do, and moderately well-educated man, who had read and was enraptured with Hölderlin's *Hyperion*. He and his family treated their demented boarder with kindness and even respect, and the poet responded with appreciation and gratitude. He remained with the Zimmer household for the rest of his life, living in a tower adjoined to the house, which afforded a view of the beautiful countryside around Tübingen. His mother paid for his upkeep, assisted by an annuity from the government.

Hölderlin lived on for nearly forty years and never recovered his sanity. When speaking, he seemed usually unable to follow a line of thought beyond a sentence or two, whereupon he would customarily lapse into gibberish. His manners, especially on meeting strangers, were extravagantly, even ludicrously courtly.[29] He preferred to address people, even old friends, by elaborate titles such as "Your Lordship," "Your Grace," or "Your Holiness." In his letters, also, even in those addressed to his mother, one is struck by the elaborate formality and the ceremonial tone. He frequently signed the letters as he signed many of his latest poems with an exotic pseudonym, such as "Buonarotti" or "Scardanelli." No one who met him in those final decades of his life doubted his insanity.[30]

Some of Hölderlin's old friends, a few of the younger generation of poets, and many simply curious people came to visit (or gawk at) the insane man. However, the most important and beneficial visitor for Hölderlin himself was a Tübingen student and aspiring writer named Wilhelm Waiblinger. He was fascinated by Hölderlin and his tragic fate and, in order both to benefit him and to observe him closely, became Hölderlin's closest companion for about four years in the 1820s. His attention had a good effect on Hölderlin, who generally seemed more relaxed and cheerful in his presence. All the while Waiblinger was carefully observing and analyzing his behavior and learning as much as possible about his past life by reading his works and talking with Zimmer and others. As a result, he was able to write the first biography of Hölderlin, *Friedrich Hölderlins Leben, Dichtung, und Wahnsinn*, which today remains a principal source of our knowledge of Hölderlin's life and behavior in the long period of his insanity.[31] The book was published in 1831, a year after Waiblinger's death.

Hölderlin himself outlived all the important people in his life. Sinclair died in 1815, while attending the Congress of Vienna. He had never seen Hölderlin again after the poet's departure from Homburg in 1806. Neither had Hölderlin's mother, although she lived only a short distance from her son in Nürtingen. She died in 1828 and, in her will, left the largest portion of her estate to be used for Hölderlin's further subsistence.

When Zimmer died in 1838, his daughter, whom Hölderlin called "Blessed Virgin Lotte" and who had always treated him with kindness and affection, took over the care of the poet.

Hölderlin died on June 7, 1843, at the age of seventy-three, presumably of lung congestion. The death was apparently quite sudden; he had not been seriously ill or bedridden, and there was reportedly no suffering. Present at the burial service in the Tübingen cemetery were a few relatives and a number of students and professors from the university. Aside from Hölderlin's future biographer Christoph Schwab, who made a brief oration at the grave, there were no literary celebrities in attendance—an ironic circumstance when one considers that on the one hundredth anniversary of his death, in the midst of the Second World War, he was ceremoniously hailed by the German literary and academic establishments as one of the fatherland's greatest poets. Joseph Goebbels represented the Führer at festivities commemorating the founding of a "Hölderlin Society."[32]

Chapter Two
Early Poetry

Hölderlin's earliest verse dates from his school days at Denkendorf, and what was probably his earliest preserved poem, "Dankgedicht an die Lehrer," was written when he was fourteen.[1] It expresses a student's gratitude (at that age quite possibly sincere) toward his clerical instructors at the junior seminary. Like much of his early poetry, this specimen is written in rhymed quatrains and belongs to a genre very popular in late eighteenth-century German verse, the so-called Klopstockian ode, a form adapted by Klopstock from the Greek and Latin Alcaic and Sapphic ode forms. Hölderlin had encountered the form not only in Klopstock but also in the more derivative poetry of such regional poets as Friedrich Matthisson and D. C. Schubart. The genre provided a versatile mode of expression for a wide variety of conventional attitudes and sentiments: praise (as here), religious musings, feelings of love or friendship, and meditations on abstract qualities or ideals. The young Hölderlin in his earliest poetic apprenticeship composed odes on all these topics.

Hölderlin continued to write poetry after he entered the Tübingen Stift, and most of the poems of his first years there are stylistically and thematically akin to those written earlier. Two poems of this period owe their existence to the "Dichterbund" Hölderlin shared with two of his closest friends at the seminary, Christian Ludwig Neuffer and Rudolf Magenau. "Lied der Freundschaft" and "Lied der Liebe" were both written to be sung at festive meetings of the group. The first celebrates the spiritual values of friendship in an extravagant manner reminiscent of a number of Hölderlin's earlier poems; here, emphasis is on friendship's ability to summon the spirits of ancient German heroes to fill today's youth with heroic courage. In "Lied der Liebe," however, we find expressed, probably for the first time in Hölderlin's poetry, an ideal central to his most important works. This is the concept of a divine world harmony, which Hölderlin inherited from Leibnitz and (more directly) from Heinse and Schiller—that the universe is a living whole, with all parts and aspects harmonized in perfect unity.[2] For Hölderlin, here as elsewhere, the vital cohesive force of this All-Unity is the power of love. The song thus praises

the cosmic efficacy of love in a meter and tone virtually identical with that
employed by Schiller's "An die Freude" in celebrating the power of joy.
Thus, the poet exhorts his friends:

> Singt den Jubel, Schwestern! Brüder!
> Festgeschlungen! Hand in Hand!
> Singt das heiligste der Lieder
> Von dem hohen Wesenband!
> Steigt hinauf am Rebenhügel,
> Blickt hinab ins Schattental!
> Überall der Liebe Flügel,
> Wonnerauschend überall! (1:110)

(Sing jubilation, sisters, brothers, joined closely hand in hand! Sing the holiest
of songs about the high Union of Being! Climb up to the vineyard hill, look
down into the shady valley! Everywhere the wings of Love [fly] thundering
ecstasy everywhere!)

The song then proceeds to praise the ability of cosmic love to harmonize all
aspects of the natural world.

   As critics have pointed out, a similar concept of universal love finds
expression in "Hymne an den Genius Griechenlands," Hölderlin's first
noteworthy statement of attitude toward ancient Greece.[3] The "Genius"
or ruling spirit of the Greek people is here deemed to be the spirit of love
itself: not only brotherly love in the Christian sense but the cosmic force
binding all things (men included) into harmony. The appraisal of Greece
first articulated in this fragmentary poem will be developed in much
greater complexity in such major works as *Hyperion,* "Brot und Wein,"
and "Der Archipelagus."

   The topic of cosmic love or harmony is also central to "Hymne an die
Göttin der Harmonie" (late 1790 or early 1791), the first of the series
known as "Hymns to the Ideals of Mankind." As already noted, these
hymns are strongly influenced by Schiller's philosophical essays and especially by his poetry. Wilhelm Michel observes that these and related
poems are radically different from much of Hölderlin's earlier poetry.[4]
Whereas most of his adolescent verses were personal, subjective meditations on his own thoughts, sentiments, desires, and frustrations, spoken
from the viewpoint of a personal self, the "I" declaiming the Tübingen
hymns seems to have virtually no connection with the historical Friedrich
Hölderlin. Rather it is the voice of an impersonal prophet or priest

proclaiming to mankind in general the glorious truths he has perceived. The tone this voice assumes, unfortunately, often appears hysterically elated, strident, and insufferably bombastic—as if the author were straining (unsuccessfully) to convince himself as well as his intended audience of the veracity and cosmic significance of his message. Of all Hölderlin's poetry, these hymns are thus likely to prove most repellent to a modern reader. Yet one should attempt to read them with sympathy and understanding, not only because of their significance in the context of Hölderlin's intellectual and poetic development, but because, as Michel remarks, they are not (as may appear) rhymed philosophical essays but the poet's actual attempts to invoke the (usually personified) ideals and to summon them to inform his mind and life. In that respect, they might actually be regarded as hymns in the usual religious sense. And they were undoubtedly intended to be sung as hymns at festive meetings between Hölderlin and his fellow-poets.

The "Goddess of Harmony" addressed in the first hymn is Urania, traditionally the muse of astronomy and often identified with the Heavenly Aphrodite, goddess or personification of universal love-harmony. In the hymn's first stanza, setting the ecstatic tone of the entire poem, the poet proclaims his approach to her:

> Froh, als könnt' ich Schöpfungen beglücken,
> Kühn, als huldigten die Geister mir,
> Nahet, in dein Heiligtum zu blicken,
> Hocherhab'ne, meine Liebe dir;
> Schon erglüht der wonnetrunkne Seher
> Von den Ahndungen der Herrlichkeit
> Ha, und deinem Götterschosse näher
> Höhnt des Siegers Fahne Grab and Zeit. (1:130)

(Happily, as if I could bless creations, boldly, as if the spirits revered me, my love approaches you to look into your sanctuary, Most Exalted One! The seer, drunk with bliss, is already aglow with the presentiments of splendor, and, ah, nearer to your divine womb the victor's flag mocks grave and time.)

As the speaker boldly approaches her "womb," Urania fills him with ever more exalted "inspiration"; the eternal source of all beauty and sublimity, she is hailed in the second stanza as "Urania, queen of the world." Urania's special worshippers should constitute a fraternal "priesthood," under whose guidance all earthly dissonances (such as political and social injustices) would be swept away. A fully harmonious human community, governed by love, would then be in tune with Urania's all-pervasive cosmic harmony.

"Hymne an die Schönheit" celebrates ideal beauty in a manner similar in tone and format to the previous poem's celebration of harmony. This time, it is beauty that is personified and addressed as Urania. Hölderlin, in keeping with the Platonic tradition, regarded such transcendental ideals as the good, the beautiful, the true, and the harmonious as different aspects of the same metaphysical reality.[5] There are two different poems entitled "Hymne an die Freiheit"; in each freedom is, like harmony and beauty, personified and addressed as a goddess. Each hymn has an introductory section spoken by the poet's persona, a middle section spoken by the goddess of freedom, and a concluding section again spoken by the poetic persona. Other poems of Hölderlin's later Tübingen years that might also be classified as hymns include the overtly political "Hymne an die Menschheit," which envisages a liberated humanity approaching perfection, hymns to love and friendship, and a festive hymn to the "spirit of youth" ("Hymne an den Genius der Jugend").

The years immediately following Hölderlin's departure from the seminary (1794–95) were not conducive to the writing of poetry. During this time the poet was being distracted by the rigors of his first tutorial job and by his equally rigorous (and poetically debilitating) study of Kant and Fichte. What time remained for literary work was devoted chiefly to his labors on the early versions of *Hyperion*. The most significant poem of this period, "An die Natur," shows the negative effect of Fichtean philosophy. Fichte's stress on the radical opposition of self and world had convinced the poet that he could never again achieve his youthful pantheistic rapport with the divine life of nature.[6] The poem is a poignant expression of regret over this loss. In 1796 Hölderlin wrote yet another poem under the influence of Fichtean philosophy. "An Herkules," however, reflects the most positive aspect of Fichte's doctrine. The poet here hails the legendary Hercules as the source of inspiration for his own heroic struggles against the world. And in this poem the author expresses confidence at soon attaining success in his endeavors.[7] In the last stanza he speaks of joining the demigod in Olympus, thereby attaining the "immortality" he has long promised himself.

This highly atypical Hölderlin poem undoubtedly reflects not only Fichteanism but the poet's unusual euphoria at the time, the happiness he had discovered in his relation with Susette Gontard, as well as his feelings of triumph at nearing the completion of *Hyperion*. It can be said that during his Frankfurt years Hölderlin experienced a general emotional and spiritual rebirth, so that his literary work flourished accordingly. Moreover, in technique some of his poetry now shows striking improvement over his earlier verse. A number of poems and fragments, addressed to Susette under the name "Diotima," explore and celebrate the significance of their relationship. The most important of these exists in three versions, the first two of which resemble the old Tübingen hymns in tone, style, and versification. In the second version, for example, the poet uses a stanzaic form similar to that employed in "Hymne an die Göttin der Harmonie," and addresses Diotima in a tone of awestruck ecstasy previously evinced by the goddess Urania. He declares that his earlier concept of Urania had actually been an anticipation of the divine principle now manifest and incarnate in her. Just as Urania was able to impose order on primeval Chaos, so Diotima, herself harmoniously intact despite the chaotic world, may bring peace and harmony to the poet's troubled soul. The concluding stanza of the third version of "Diotima," in its euphony and in the vividness and resonance of its imagery, might be considered superior to most of Hölderlin's previous verse:

> Wie dein Vater und der meine,
> Der in heitrer Majestät
> Über seinem Eichenhaine
> Dort in lichter Höhe geht,
> Wie er in die Meereswogen,
> Wo die kühle Tiefe blaut,
> Steigend von des Himmels Bogen,
> Klar und still herunterschaut:
> So will ich aus Götterhöhen
> Neu geweiht in schön'rem Glük,
> Froh zu singen und zu sehen,
> Nun zu Sterblichen zurück. (1:222)

(Like your Father and mine, who in serene majesty walks there in radiant height above his oak grove, as he, descending from the vault of heaven, in clarity and silence looks down into the sea-waves where the cool depths are blue: thus will I, newly consecrated in more beautiful happiness, joyously to sing and to see, return now to mortals from the gods' heights.)

This passage contains one of Hölderlin's earliest references to a paternal sky-god who will later be addressed as Father Aether. More significantly, the nature imagery in this passage reflects the poet's new sense of rapport with the natural world. His apprehension of Diotima-Susette as the incarnation of harmonious divine Life had enabled him to transcend the Fichtean doctrine of the radical alienation of the self from nature. Direct intuition of the divinity present in the soul of "Diotima" had given him new assurance that he could intuitively sense and achieve rapport with the divine soul of the universe. Whereas in Tübingen the truth of pantheism had been a strongly held intellectual conviction for the poet, it was now an intuitive certainty; and the mystical ecstasies for which he had unsuccessfully striven in the Tübingen hymns could now be attained as apparently authentic experiences.

Hölderlin's poetry of this time (as well as much of the prose in *Hyperion*) gives evidence of this new assurance in dealing with the natural world. The diction and imagery of most of his earlier poetry (particularly the hymns) had been laden with "poetic" artifice in the worst eighteenth-century tradition. References to natural objects usually occurred in conventional, often hackneyed, similes and metaphors intended to reinforce specific rhetorical points. Now, in the best poetry of his Frankfurt years, nature images begin to be employed with great skill in a manner that appeals to the reader's visual imagination and evokes subtle emotional responses, so that one senses their value as true symbols rather than mere decorative embellishments. Thus Hölderlin began to work into his poetry a type of diction and imagery that, at virtually the same time, was being devised by Wordsworth and Coleridge in England.

Several poems of his Frankfurt years, composed in hexameters, show the influence of an older contemporary, Friedrich Leopold, Count von Stolberg, whose own poetry was written in stylistic emulation of the so-called Homeric hymns, Greek poems addressed to the gods.[8] These Hölderlin poems are especially notable for the density and vividness of their nature imagery. One of them, "Die Eichbäume" (written probably in 1796), achieves an empathy with natural objects comparable to that attained by Rilke in his "Dinggedichte."[9] Hölderlin also manages to invest them with symbolic meaning: their sturdy independence represents the radical "freedom" to which he would aspire if "love" did not bring him back to "social life" ("geselliges Leben") corresponding to the domesticity of the gardens.

Hölderlin's two most significant poems composed in this style are "Der Wanderer" and "An den Aether" (both written in 1797). As the first of these can be considered an elegy, it will be discussed in a later chapter. "An den Aether" is perhaps the first poem in which Hölderlin's paternal deity, Father Aether, is addressed by that name. As generally for Hölderlin, "Aether" is here ultimately identical with air, one of the four ancient elements (the others being earth, fire, and water) which some Greeks, such as the philosopher Empedocles, considered divine presences or substances.[10] There are also precedents among the ancients for viewing Aether or its natural "home" or locus, the blue sky, as a paternal divinity.[11] The sky, like Zeus (its anthropomorphic equivalent), rules *over* the other gods. In this poem, likewise, the sky is the true home of Aether. But Hölderlin, like a number of Greek thinkers, also regards Aether as an element pervading all living things. It is the air we breathe; and, according to the poem, the presence of this divine element within our souls makes all creatures yearn for its native region, the heavens. The poem affirms and celebrates this yearning. Moreover, since Aether is itself an all-pervasive divinity, we can regard this poem as further evidence that Hölderlin had by now triumphantly overcome his last Fichtean scruple over the validity of pantheistic mysticism.

Aside from a number of epigrams, a few occasional poems, and a brief poem ("Da ich ein Knabe war . . .") expressing nostalgia for childhood, most of the rest of Hölderlin's Frankfurt (or Homburg) poetry consists of odes modeled directly after Greek Alcaic or Asclepidean odes; these will be discussed in a later chapter devoted to the genre. Finally, we might mention here a curious work written in 1799, the epistolary verse narrative, "Emilie vor ihrem Brauttag." It will be recalled that Hölderlin was then trying to found a magazine aimed at a moderately educated female readership. This lengthy narrative was written and submitted to a prospective publisher as an example of the type of story that would form the bulk of the magazine's material. In it (he explained to the publisher) he intended to present in his protagonist Emilie "the character of a really noble, splendid girl."[12] In this attempt to write for an extensive, less sophisticated audience, Hölderlin failed completely. The story is insipid and tedious to the point of being unreadable. It represents the last instance (before his final madness) of any Hölderlin poem that can unquestionably be judged an esthetic failure.

Chapter Three

Hyperion

It must be admitted that Hölderlin's novel, *Hyperion, oder der Eremit in Griechenland (Hyperion: Or the Hermit in Greece)* poses serious problems both of comprehension and of appreciation. Its protagonist, a young modern Greek, seemingly overreacts to people and situations, and his feelings move with great frequency and rapidity from elation to despondency. In keeping with these extreme changes in mood, the protagonist devises a great variety of apparently contradictory metaphysical hypotheses, all expounded with great eloquence and enthusiasm. It is not surprising, then, that the majority of its readers have, until fairly recently, regarded *Hyperion* as an unstructured lyrical novel to be read and appreciated chiefly for the 'poetic' qualities of its prose. Only in the last several decades have critics succeeded in establishing that the novel is in fact a highly structured and complex work, an astute psychological study of the intellectual and emotional maturation of its protagonist.[1]

As noted in the introductory chapter, Hölderlin subjected the *Hyperion* material to many revisions before completing the novel. He began to work on it in 1792, while still at Tübingen; nothing has been preserved of these earliest sketches. The first extant version, written in 1794, was published in Schiller's journal *Die Neue Thalia* under the title "Fragment von Hyperion." Its preface expounds a number of ideas that many critics have sought to apply to the final version of the novel.

The preface states that there are "two ideals of our existence."[2] One is the "condition of highest simplicity," in which our needs are harmonized with each other, our abilities, and the external world through a natural, preconscious "organization"; such simple harmony is implicitly that found in plants, animals, and small children. The other ideal is the "condition of highest development ['Bildung']," in which a similar harmony has been achieved among more complicated needs and abilities "through the organization which we are able to give to ourselves." All men must run an "eccentric course" ("exzentrische Bahn") from the point of "more or less pure simplicity" to the point of "more or less complete development." Critics have speculated variously regarding the

22

meaning of the phrase "eccentric course," the exact character of the "eccentricity," and whether such a course can be discerned in the completed novel.[3] Such speculations are highly interesting, but it might be most useful to interpret "eccentric" here merely as "erratic" and to refrain from applying the concept to the completed novel, as the phrase does not appear in the final preface.

During the winter of 1794–95, Hölderlin composed the blank-verse "metrical version" of *Hyperion,* and in the latter half of 1795, he was writing what Friedrich Beissner terms the "penultimate version" of the novel, which returns to epistolary form. Of interest here is a new preface, which develops some of the principal ideas of the earlier one.[4] The author apologizes for the vacillations and seeming contradictions in Hyperion's character by again remarking that the protagonist, like everyone else, must traverse an "eccentric course," for "there is no other way possible from childhood to completion." He then explains:

Die selige Einigkeit, das Sein, im einzigen Sinne des Worts, ist für uns verloren und wir müssen es erlieren, wen wir es erstreben, erringn solten. Wir reissen uns los vom friedlichen εν και παν der Welt, um es herzustellen, durch uns Selbst. Wir sind zerfallen mit der Natur. . . . (3:236)

(Blissful unity, being in the only [true] sense of the word, is lost for us and we had to lose it [true being] if we are to strive, to struggle for it. We tear ourselves loose from the peaceful εν και παν [One and All] of the world in order to establish it through ourselves. We have fallen away from Nature. . . .)

Hölderlin here sees man's initial condition as one of integration in the serene All-Unity of the cosmos. With the coming of consciousness, we disrupt this preconscious unity by differentiating our subjectivity from the objective world; or, as Fichte would say, we posit an "I" and a "Not-I." However, whereas Fichte would demand that the self should incessantly struggle to dominate the nonself, Hölderlin deplores the necessity of such a struggle. He rather feels that we should strive to reestablish the original harmony between ourselves and nature, but on a *conscious* level. Thus, he continues:

Jenen ewigen Widerstreit zwischen unserem Selbst und der Welt zu endigen, den Frieden alles Friedens, der höher ist, denn alle Vernunft, den wiederzu-

bringen, uns mit der Natur zu vereinigen zu Einem unendlichen Ganzen, das ist
das Ziel all unseres Strebens. . . . (3:236)

(To end that conflict between our Self and the world, to bring back the peace of
all peace that is higher than all reason, to unite ourselves with Nature in one
infinite whole, that is the goal of all our striving. . . .)

The beauty of the natural world supplies us with a model of perfected
harmony, encouraging us to work toward a society where all men will be
united in a harmony whose beauty would rival nature: "a new realm . . .
where Beauty is queen."

After further revision, the first volume of the final version of the novel
was submitted for publication and it appeared in April 1797. The second
volume appeared together with a reissue of the first in the autumn of 1799.
As an epistolary novel, the finished *Hyperion* had important eighteenth-
century predecessors in Rousseau's *Julie: ou la nouvelle Héloïse* and in
Goethe's *Die Leiden des jungen Werthers.* In those novels, however, most of
the letters are written by protagonists immediately or soon after the
events they describe, almost in the manner of a diary; they convey a sense
of immediacy and involvement with the narrated events. In Hölderlin's
novel, however, the protagonist does not begin the narration until the
events themselves, drawn from Hyperion's earlier life, have been completed.[5] The letters are addressed to Bellarmin, a friend whom Hyperion
had met while studying in Germany after the collapse of a revolution in
Greece. Written at the urging of the friend, Hyperion's letters are
composed from a perspective detached in time and usually at some
emotional distance from the events recounted.

It is now generally held that in the process of retelling his life story the
narrator gains an increased understanding of himself and of life in general.
Hölderlin states in the final preface to the novel that its theme is the
"resolution of the dissonances in a certain character." No mention is made
of the two ideal states of harmony or of any "eccentric course" between
them. Rather than seeking to trace any pattern of eccentricity, then, an
analysis of the final version of the novel should accordingly focus on the
dissonances within Hyperion and examine how, if at all, they achieve
"resolution." One must also take care to distinguish between the deeds,
thoughts, and feelings of the older narrator and those of the younger man
whose story is being told. As the final version is divided into four sections
(two "volumes," each consisting of two "books"), I will consider each
section in turn.

The first two letters of the novel are concerned not with the past but with the narrator's immediate present. Just returned to Greece from Germany and determined to lead the life of a hermit, Hyperion first remarks that his fatherland gives him both "joy" (because of its natural beauty) and "sorrow" (because of its degeneracy and continued enslavement by the Turks). His participation in a recent insurrection having made him a hunted outlaw in his own country, he laments that his "business on earth" is finished—his political efforts wasted and his beloved "far and dead." His only recourse now is to return to the "arms of Nature, the unchanging, the calm, and the beautiful." He thus experiences "Unity with everything that lives." This return "to the all of Nature" involves a "blessed self-forgetfulness" beyond any concern with "virtue," "reason," or "thoughts," and beyond the powers of "Destiny" or even "death." And yet, Hyperion laments, one "moment of reflection" is enough to cast him down into the loneliness of finite consciousness. Hyperion here castigates the skeptical teachings of critical philosophy, which rendered such pantheistic ecstasies metaphysically disreputable through rejecting the assumptions of pantheistic belief.[6] Thus, he laments, his study of philosophy has "spoiled everything" for him. The second letter concludes with the more general complaint that man "is a god when he dreams but a beggar when he reflects," thus underscoring the radical "dissonances" still existing in the psyche of the narrator.[7]

In the third letter, Hyperion, at his correspondent's request, begins to recount the story of his life. Childhood is described in the customary romantic fashion as a time of undisturbed inner peace, the harmonious "simplicity" of the earlier preface: the child, because as yet unreflective, lives in blissful unity with the world. Yet, Hyperion continues, the first awakening from this state can also be glorious in aspirations which seem on the verge of fulfillment. In Hyperion's case, guidance was supplied by a wise man named Adamas, who seems to be an idealized composite of some of Hölderlin's earlier mentors.[8] Adamas is a philosopher and educator who comes to Greece in search of some living remnant of its former genius. He finds his ideal subject in the young Hyperion, in whom he awakens "the omnipotence of undivided inspiration," which he channels into enthusiasm for knowledge and zeal for reawakening the ancient genius of the Greeks. Adamas ultimately leaves Hyperion in search of a "nation of rare excellence" in the "depths of Asia," with whom he could presumably enjoy pedagogical success on a larger scale.

The following letters tell how the young Hyperion left his parents and his native island of Tina for the city of Smyrna in Asia Minor, where he indulged his obsession with Greek antiquity. He soon, however, became disgusted with the degeneracy of the people of Smyrna and began to spend most of his days in excursions in the countryside, where he frequently saw a young man of great stature and beauty. One day Hyperion is set upon by two robbers but is able to fight them off. He later encounters the young man, Alabanda, and learns that Alabanda, who had been riding in search of Hyperion, had earlier met and defeated the same two robbers. In this improbably heroic first encounter, they immediately declare their enthusiasm for each other and the intensity of their shared political idealism.[9] Both intensely detest the existing political and social order and share a revolutionary zeal. The Greeks, they agree, should be ruled by a brilliantly heroic elite, and the recalcitrance of the populace must be disposed of without compunction. Only once does Hyperion timidly remark that if possible one might dispose of it "gently"; he is generally swept away by Alabanda's violent enthusiasm. The conversation ends in a joint pledge of eternal brotherhood in a victorious struggle to "save the fatherland."

Later, however, the basic disagreements between the embittered Alabanda and the more idealistic Hyperion become manifest. Hyperion objects that Alabanda allots too much importance to the state as a means of implementing social reform. Reform, he insists, cannot be legislated; instead it must come about freely and spontaneously through mass inspiration. Mankind will then constitute a "new church," a union of individuals all governed by divine inspiration. As Hyperion becomes more and more enthusiastic, Alabanda interrupts him with a sarcastic remark, and at that point several men enter the room in which they are conversing. We later learn that they, with Alabanda, are members of a terrorist conspiracy known as the Band of Nemesis and represent the violently destructive aspects of Alabanda's politics. Hyperion is repelled by the asperity and coldness in the strangers' faces and horrified that Alabanda should associate with them. The next day he indignantly takes Alabanda to task and demands apology. Alabanda refuses, and their mutual pride compels them to quarrel and break up. Hyperion immediately lapses into deep depression and decides to relinquish his ambitions to reform the world; instead he will return to Tina and, he hopes, to the "innocence" of a secluded, bucolic existence.

The remaining epistles of part one of the first volume are generally devoted to Hyperion's gradual recovery from his depression. He eventually writes to Alabanda, hoping to renew their friendship, but when he receives no response, even after three letters, he lapses again into despondency and succumbs to a philosophy of nihilism, the result (the narrator remarks) of the destructive intellectual forces that moved him.

The second section of the novel begins with a description of the narrator's present situation. He is now living, still as a hermit, on Salamis, an island famous as the site of the great naval battle in which the Greeks defeated the Persians. In the second letter of this section, the narrator announces that he feels he has now achieved sufficient harmony and strength within himself to speak of the central episode of his life, his relationship with Diotima.

A friend, Notara, invited the young Hyperion to come to live near him on the island of Kalauria. Hyperion accepts the invitation, and when he arrives in Kalauria, he succumbs to the joyous, ethereal mood that seems to possess all creatures that day. He feels as if he were being led by an invisible power into Diotima's presence. The narrator then tells in glowing terms what Diotima had meant to him. She was for him the equivalent of the beatific vision, "the only thing my soul sought after, and the fulfillment that we project up beyond the stars." She was the living embodiment of the absolute beauty that all men desire and to which he now, after her death, has devoted his life. She, like her namesake in *The Symposium,* had shown the way to its attainment.

He then describes his first meeting with her. She and Hyperion, as kindred spirits, were at once enraptured with each other, and after very few words, they launched into a joint philosophical-poetic celebration of "the life of the earth." The following letters celebrate various aspects of Diotima's personality: her song, which evoked the "peace of heaven"; her heart, most "at home" among the flowers; even her culinary skills, in which Hyperion discerns a spiritual dimension.

Their relationship, the narrator declares, was based on the polarity of their natures, Diotima was "divinely self-sufficient," wholly without needs; her peace was a constant source of solace to his restless heart. He had nothing to offer her except feelings "full of wild contradictions, full of bleeding memories"—or "boundless love with its thousand cares, its thousand raging hopes." Thus what others have sought in the promised bliss of an afterlife, he has already known on earth:

Ich stand vor ihr, und hört und sah den Frieden des Himmels, und mitten im seufzenden Chaos erschien mir Urania. . . . Sie war mein Lethe, diese Seele, mein heiliger Lethe, woraus ich die Vergessenheit des Daseins trank, dass ich vor ihr stand, wie ein Unsterblicher. (3:58–59)

(I stood before her, and heard and saw the peace of heaven, and in the midst of sighing chaos appeared to me Urania. . . .she was my Lethe, this soul, my holy Lethe, out of which I drank the forgetfulness of existence, so that I stood before her as an immortal.)

In the following letters, the narrator's renewed grief over the death of Diotima, reawakened through the telling of his story, moves him to visit the vicinity of Diotima's grave, where he gives full vent to his misery. He then resumes the account of their relationship and recalls an evening he and Diotima spent in the company of some friends in Kalauria. The conversation turned to the topic of friendship, and Hyperion, reminded of his aborted friendship with Alabanda, delivered an enthusiastic speech which developed a view of history heavily influenced by the writings of Schiller and conceptually related to the ideas Hölderlin expounds in the early preface of the novel.[10] Mankind as a whole began its existence in childlike harmony, a "vegetative happiness" ("Pflanzenglück"). Through maturation the human race developed a kind of intellectual ferment which has now resulted in a discordant chaos. The real beauty that had once been present in the structures and conduct of human life has now taken refuge in the mind; it is present to us now only as an ideal. But this ideal of beauty can be seized upon by an elite of young men who, in the enthusiasms of heroic friendship, can bring about a rejuvenation of mankind initiating the second age of life of the world—corresponding to the "new church" hailed in Hyperion's earlier conversation with Alabanda.

Hyperion then recounts how he told Diotima the story of his friendships with Adamas and Alabanda and how, with the termination of the friendships, the gods hurled him "from heaven to earth." Diotima immediately diagnoses why these relationships affected him so deeply:

Du wolltest keine Menschen, glaube mir, du wolltest eine Welt. Den Verlust von allen goldenen Jahrhunderten, so wie du sie, zusammengedrängt in Einem glücklichen Moment, empfändest, den Geist von allen Geistern bessrer Zeit, die Kraft von allen Kräften der Heroen, das sollte dir ein Einzelner, ein Mensch ersetzen! (3:67)

(You did not want human beings, believe me, you wanted a world. The loss of all golden centuries, just as you felt them compressed in one happy moment, the spirit of all spirits of better time, the power of all powers of heroes—an individual, a human being was to replace them for you.)

(Neither the young Hyperion nor the narrator here observes that she might be alluding to their own relationship as well.) Hyperion, she continued, is thus both rich and poor, and alternates between joy and suffering: he has "everything" in his mind as an ideal but "nothing" in actuality. He thus lives solely in a world of fantasy and cannot confront reality. Hyperion, elated at this appraisal of himself, agrees enthusiastically but predicts success in his future efforts to transform his imaginary world into actuality. In his excitement, he formally proposes marriage to Diotima, who gives no unequivocal answer but remarks that she is only "mortal," thereby suggesting that he has perhaps overvalued and hopelessly idealized her, also.

He and Diotima had by now reached an ethereally high plateau in their relationship. For a while, it seemed, the dissonances had disappeared from Hyperion's life; both he and Diotima seemed spiritually aglow like the sun. Then Diotima became somewhat more reserved; she finally confessed that she felt troubled by the force and intensity of her love for him. Her naturally harmonious, loving relationship to the things and moods of nature had yielded to a love focused on him alone, and yet all the presences of nature seem united with him. This revelation, of course, makes Hyperion more ecstatic than ever. But the narrator, who is reliving these feelings and events, must here pause, for he knows that he must soon tell how this happiness was lost and doubts if he is emotionally capable of reliving his loss.

The concluding letter of the first volume is one of the longest in the novel and is also one of the most important; some critics view it as a key to understanding the novel as a whole.[11] Although the lengthy disquisition on the cultural history of ancient Athens is presented by the protagonist Hyperion, it seems clear that it represents also the views of the narrator.

Hyperion expounds his ideas as he, Diotima, and some friends are underway on a boat from Kalaurea to visit the ruins of Athens. His lecture assumes (like the earlier speech on friendship) an analogy between the history of a people and the life of an individual. The Athenians, he declares, benefited from the slow and gradual maturation of their culture. Unlike the Spartans, who had grown precociously unruly and required strict discipline, the Athenians remained longer in childlike simplicity and innocence. Their environment offered them neither poverty nor overabundance but a "moderate prosperity." Such moderation was thus elevated to an ethical value, leading Theseus, for example, voluntarily to restrict his own royal power. Thus, Hyperion asserts:

Lasst von der Wiege an den Menschen ungestört! . . . lasst den Menschen spät erst wissen, das es Menschen, dass es irgend etwas ausser ihm gibt, denn so nur wird er Mensch. Der Mensch ist aber ein Gott, so bald er Mensch ist. Und ist er ein Gott, so ist er schön. (3:79)

(Leave a human being undisturbed from the cradle on. . . . let a human being learn only late that there are [other] human beings, that there is anything outside of himself, for only thus does he become a human being. But a human being is a god as soon as he is a human being. And if he is a god, he is beautiful.)

In equating full humanity with divinity, Hyperion is espousing the humanistic doctrine that, in a world where the Deity is the immanent life force or soul, man, being the most spiritual entity, is the highest conscious realization of this deity. And, as Hyperion elaborates, this highest realization occurs in the experience of absolute beauty, an experience achieved most fully by the Athenians.

The first product of the experience of absolute beauty is art, particularly the arts of poetry and sculpture in which the Greeks depicted their gods, actually objectifying their own spiritual beauty in order to feel it better. The second, derivative product was Greek religion, which Hyperion defines as "love of the beautiful"—that is, love of the beautiful gods first imagined by artists. Thus Hyperion concludes that both art and religion were "true children of eternal Beauty," identical with "completed human nature"; both are ultimately (though benignly) narcissistic. When asked how this theory accounts for the development of Athenian philosophy, Hyperion replies that only a poetic disposition such as the Athenians possessed was capable of producing great philosophy. All true philosophers must at least at one time have had an experience of absolute beauty, a state of highest "inspiration" in which all "powers" are brought into play and most intensely "harmonized" with one another.[12] The experience is best defined analytically by Heraclitus as "the One differentiated in itself." This definition of beauty was virtually the founding insight of Greek philosophy, with its fundamental concern for the relationship between the concepts of unity and multiplicity.

At this point Hyperion concludes his lecture, for the boat reaches the coast of Attica. The following day they visit the ruins of the Acropolis and the lower town, and Hyperion tells Diotima that although Athens may be dead, the "source of eternal beauty" is still present in her. Diotima replies that, instead of reposing inertly in the heaven of his love, he should return to a more active confrontation with the world, which is in need of his talents and energies. He should not have been so easily discouraged by the disappointment following his earlier political enthusiasm. The minds and souls of the "good, childish Greeks" are not an unworthy object of his efforts.

Hyperion responds enthusiastically to her challenge. Now that he has achieved harmony within himself and, through an experience of absolute beauty in his love for Diotima, has attained full humanity, he feels capable of leadership. He should be able to reawaken the "ancient truth," the experience and worship of beauty in the land of the Greeks, and revivify it to "new, vital youth." He would, of course, need to go abroad, Diotima tells him, to complete his education and learn the arts of leadership. Then he would return to Greece and become the visionary "educator of our nation" and "a great man."

At the beginning of the second half of the novel, Hyperion receives a letter from Alabanda, announcing that Russia has declared war on Turkey and has promised the Greeks independence if they will mount a successful rebellion against the Turks.[13] Now freed from the conspiracy that had alienated Hyperion, Alabanda calls upon him to join him in the revolutionary struggle, thus translating into reality their old dreams of heroism. Hyperion's immediate and overwhelming reaction is one of envy of his friend, and he is again possessed by his old enthusiasm for heroic action modeled after ancient examples. Diotima's reaction is, understandably, unenthusiastic. She immediately urges Hyperion not to take part, reminding him of his former decision to be the peaceful educator of his people, but he remains adamant. Diotima finally declares that she will endure his decision.

Hyperion's friend Notara approves of his undertaking and provides him with men and money. His departure takes place on a winter day at Diotima's house; all their mutual friends are present. After telling of his highly emotional, even lugubrious parting from Diotima, the narrator explains to Bellarmin that he is willing to relive the pains of his youth because it is necessary to comprehend and appreciate the totality of one's life. In recounting the often painful vicissitudes of his early life, he has paradoxically achieved a kind of "peace" based on fuller understanding of himself. Now he is going to forward to Bellarmin some letters exchanged between himself and Diotima at the time of his involvement in the insurrection.

The young Hyperion soon writes to Diotima to tell her of his joyous reunion with Alabanda; they are dearer to one another than ever. Alabanda tells Hyperion of the political and military situation: the Russians are not to be trusted, but the Greek forces probably can conquer and hold the Peloponnesus, thus securing independence for that part of Greece. Military operations soon began and the rebel army won a number of minor skirmishes. After capturing the town of Ministra, however, the troops went berserk and, on entering the town, "plundered and murdered without distinction" Greek as well as Turkish inhabitants. In attempting to put a stop to the looting and mayhem, Hyperion was wounded by one of his own soldiers. Alabanda, who rescued the wounded Hyperion from the fray, is now nursing him faithfully. The entire region has lapsed into chaos as bands of mutinous Greek soldiers go about the country murdering and pillaging. Hyperion later informs Diotima that he has given up on the Greeks and has decided to enter service with the Russian fleet. He is no longer worthy of her. The ignominious day of the battle has taken away all his youth, and he cannot bear merely to be pitied by her. The Turkish government has outlawed him like a common rebel and his father has formally disowned him.

In his next letter he announces that he has already joined the Russian navy and anticipates the following day a naval battle that, he hopes, will, like a bath, "wash off the dust" of his earthly life. In conclusion, he bids her farewell.

At the beginning of the second book of the second volume, the narrator returns to a retrospective telling of events. In the battle between the Russian and Turkish fleets, Hyperion, in a fit of suicidal energy, runs into the thick of the fray on board his ship, hoping to be killed. A Turkish sailor finally wounds him, and he becomes unconscious. Afterwards he learns that the two ships went up in flames immediately after a surgeon took him away in a lifeboat. After six days in a painful stupor, he awakens to see Alabanda at his bedside; his friend had been in assiduous attendance since the battle. Hyperion slowly convalesces and becomes again susceptible to the quiet beauty of nature. He regrets his earlier suicidal decision, for his demise would have been painful to Alabanda and Diotima. At Alabanda's urging, he decides to write Diotima a letter telling her of his survival.

Just as Hyperion begins to write, a letter arrives from Diotima responding to his farewell note. She does not fault him for his intended suicide, for she realizes that the failure of his great hope and the bestiality of his soldiers had robbed him of the will to live. Hyperion immediately responds with a letter proposing that they flee from Greece and take refuge in a secluded valley in the Alps or the Pyrenees and lead an idyllic existence.

The next letter to Bellarmin recounts Alabanda's final parting from Hyperion. Alabanda tells Hyperion that he cannot accompany him to Diotima, as Hyperion had hoped, for Alabanda is convinced that if he met her he would fall in love with her; one cannot hope to behold without loving "such a divine, undivided life." As this love would be violently disruptive, Alabanda feels he has no choice but to leave. He then tells Hyperion of how he originally came to join the terroristic Band of Nemesis, so that he took an oath and solemnly handed over his "blood and soul" to these men. He was assigned the Smyrna area, and he had been taking orders there ever since. After he had attempted to introduce Hyperion to the group, he was faced with a difficult decision: to give up his friendship with Hyperion or to leave and thus break his oath to the group. Confronted with this alternative, he preferred "the divine right of the heart," although he knew that the conspirators would eventually hunt him down and kill him as a traitor. And now he is faced with another decision. He predicts that if he were to live in the vicinity of both Hyperion and Diotima, he would eventually betray Hyperion and murder him and Diotima out of frustration for union with her. Instead, he has decided to pay retribution for his treachery to the group: he will give himself up to be judged and executed by them. In bidding farewell, Alabanda wishes Hyperion happiness in his love for Diotima.

As Hyperion waits for his own ship to Kalaurea, he consoles himself by singing a song Adamas had taught him in youth. As "Hyperions Schicksalslied," it is one of Hölderlin's best-known poems:

> Ihr wandelt droben im Licht
> Auf weichem Boden, selige Genien!
> Glänzende Götterlüfte
> Rühren euch leicht,
> Wie die Finger der Künstlerin
> Heilige Saiten.
>
> Schicksallos, wie der schlafende
> Säugling, atmen die Himmlischen;
> Keusch bewahrt
> In bescheidener Knospe,
> Blühet ewig
> Ihnen der Geist,
> Und die seligen Augen
> Blicken in stiller
> Ewiger Klarheit.

Doch uns ist gegeben,
Auf keiner Stätte zu ruhn,
Es schwinden, es fallen
Die leidenden Menschen
Blindlings von einer
Stunde zur anderen,
Wie Wasser von Klippe
Zu Klippe geworfen,
Jahr lang ins Ungewisse hinab. (3:143)

(You wander above us in the light on soft ground, blessed spirits! Gleaming divine breezes touch you gently as the artist's fingers [touch] sacred strings. Without destiny like the sleeping infant the Heavenly Ones breathe. Their minds blossom eternally, chastely preserved in the modest bud. And their blessed eyes gaze in calm, eternal clarity. But to us it is given to rest in no place; suffering human beings dizzily fall blindly from one hour to the other like water tossed from ledge to ledge for years long down into uncertainty.)

The poem contrasts the lives of gods with those of mortals. The gods lead lives of eternal, unchanging presence; they are perfect examples of the primal simplicity described in the early preface. Human beings, however, are subject to destiny and thus experience constant insecurity and uncertainty; their lives are nothing but series of unpleasant surprises.

Immediately after reciting this song, Hyperion receives a letter from Diotima, announcing that she is dying. She interprets her illness as a spiritual "fire" that is at once consuming her body and enhancing the radiance of her spirit. She denies that grief for him is causing her demise. Rather, the enthusiasms of their love had made her too "ripe"; her soul now, like an arrogant youth, disdains its mortal existence. Although she foresees Hyperion's despair, she is sure that the "Spirit" will save him. Just as he has imparted his fire to her, so he will come fully to realize for himself *her* "Olympus," the world of beauty, and will find consolation in the presences of the elemental gods of nature. Diotima herself has always been assured of man's immortality. For, she asserts, all life is one, and this unity is divine. "We separate only to be more intensely unified, more divinely peaceful with all" the universe and also "with ourselves." "We die," she declares, "in order to live." In conclusion, she comforts Hyperion with a prophecy: when he eventually recovers from his grief and has been accorded his vision of divine unity, he will become a priest of nature and will deserve the laurel crown of inspired poetry.

Accompanying Diotima's final letter is one from their friend Notara, describing how she died peacefully in her sleep the night after writing her letter. She is to be cremated and her ashes deposited in an urn on the site of her first meeting with Hyperion. Notara advises Hyperion against coming to Kalaurea.

Forced into exile, Hyperion travels first to Sicily and eventually to Germany, where he befriends Bellarmin. One of the most famous letters in the novel consists of the narrator's diatribe against "the Germans." (There is evidence from Hölderlin's correspondence that this polemic reflects some of the author's own current feelings about his country-men—particularly, we may assume, the Frankfurt bourgeoisie whose behavior and attitudes had so distressed him.) He regards the Germans as "barbarians" out of excessive rationality and discipline. Because they have no harmony or beauty within their souls, they are incapable of recognizing the beauteous harmony manifest in nature, in art, or in other people. Each German develops only those faculties, skills, and interests that are necessary to his profession and neglects all other aspects of his personality. Even their so-called virtues are acquired out of cowardly fear of authority and are cultivated with servile effort. Hyperion concludes this letter by declaring to Bellarmin that he knows he has spoken also in Bellarmin's name for all those in Germany (including the small minority of civilized Germans) who suffer as he has suffered there.

The final letter of the novel is perhaps the most controversial. Critics disagree as to how or whether it supplies an adequate conclusion, whether it succeeds in articulating a final "resolution of dissonances" within the character Hyperion as foretold in the preface, and whether the sentiments expressed in its concluding section are equally those of Hyperion, the character, and Hyperion, the narrator.[14] It has even been asked whether Hölderlin himself considered the novel finished at this point. The final words, "So I thought. More later," have led some readers, including a number of Hölderlin's contemporaries, to assume that a third volume was planned.[15]

The letter follows immediately upon Hyperion's diatribe castigating Germany and (implicitly) the modern world at its worst. It is remark-able, then, that Germany is here the setting of an ecstatic mystical experience. Although Hyperion wanted to get out of Germany as soon as possible, he was detained by a "heavenly spring." He again yearned to return to the childlike state of simplicity described in the early preface, a state of peace in unthinkingly blissful union with all being. Such complete return to simplicity, however, is not advocated in any of the novel's prefaces; here, submissiveness to nature serves merely as the precondition to a mystical experience which shows in a complex way *how* man is related to the all. Alone in a beautiful rural setting, Hyperion discovers that his love for the springtime is arousing an incomprehensible longing in him. He calls out, "Diotima . . . where are you?" And he seems to hear the voice of Diotima herself, who answers, "I am with my own . . . with your own, those whom the errant human mind does not recognize." On hearing this, Hyperion falls into a swoon and, when he awakens, asks himself how he might decipher this riddle.

Looking back on the experience, the narrator declares that his mental processes during the trance were so intense and self-consuming as to defy recollection. Such an admission might be taken as a confession that the following reconstruction of the ideas in the trance is wholly inadequate. But it may also be interpreted (as one critic suggests) as hyperbole indicating, rather, that the reconstruction must necessarily to a large extent be the invention as well as the recollection of the present narrator. We might therefore have reason to take the strongly stated ideas of this section of the letter as representing the opinions of the narrator, not merely the younger Hyperion.[16]

The reconstruction takes the form of a prayer to nature, here as always regarded as the divine life of the universe. Hyperion now for the first time recognizes the truth in Diotima's earlier words to him: they are not separated but unified in this all-encompassing life, "living notes" harmonizing in nature's "euphony." Ultimately all things originate out of joy and end in peace. He then makes the novel's final pronouncement on the topic of "dissonance":

Wie der Zwist der Liebenden, sind die Dissonanzen der Welt. Versöhnung ist mitten im Streit und alles Getrennte findet sich wieder. Es scheiden und kehren im Herzen die Adern und einiges, ewiges, glühendes Leben is Alles. (3:160)

(The dissonances of the world are like the quarrel of lovers. Reconciliation is in the midst of strife, and all things divided find each other again. The veins depart from and return to the heart, and a unified, eternal, glowing life is All.)

The significance of these statements has been vigorously disputed by critics. Although other interpretations are possible, it is perhaps most plausible, in terms of the entire novel, to see a shift of emphasis here from the dissonances within an individual psyche to the dissonances within the cosmos as a whole. We have observed that Hyperion, as an individual, has been markedly unsuccessful in his attempts to resolve the discords within himself—his violent shifts of mood, even of philosophical and political opinion, throughout the novel have attested to this inability. Here, however, he seems able to see how dissonances are resolved within the universe, viewed as one complex living entity. Two images are used: a lovers' quarrel, in which reconciliation actually is achieved in the process of altercation; and a circulatory system in which all things, like drops of blood, are separated only eventually to be reunited. The problem of dissonance, then, is solved not by attending to the difficulties (ultimately insignificant) within the psyche of the individual, but by regarding the individual himself as a mutable but ultimately indestructible part of a diverse but ultimately unified living whole which is eternal and benign. Dissonances within the whole of nature are always arising but are always unfailingly resolved. It is only this cosmic harmony that can resolve individual dissonances, and in terms of this harmony they cease to have any significance whatsoever.

It might also be pointed out here that just as this passage resolves the problem of dissonance by raising it to a universal level, so it alters and resolves the problem of beauty. It will be recalled how Hyperion's obsession with beauty has dominated the novel. Ancient Greece provided an example of a society in which the individual attained complete inner harmony, thus achieving beauty of soul and, in optimal cases, a vision of absolute beauty. In Diotima, Hölderlin encountered a contemporary who had achieved such harmony and thus could provide him with a realization of the absolute, which he worshipped in her. Henceforth he could perceive the full beauty of the external world through her eyes. When he offered to marry her, she urged him rather to commit himself to "educating" the modern Greeks, raising them to full perception of the beautiful and consequently enabling them to reconstitute a beautiful society.

At Alabanda's prompting, however, he reverts to his earlier dream of achieving such a society through political action. When the venture fails, he abandons all hope in society and seeks to return to his idyllic personal obsession with Diotima. She, however, is dying—chiefly, she explains, from a kind of spiritual consumption through obsession with Hyperion's own concept of the absolute. In her final letter to him, she urges upon him a poetic vocation as priest of "divine Nature." And, in the concluding letter of the novel, the reawakening of his responsiveness to the beauty of nature occasions both an imagined message from Diotima herself and his own interpretation of nature (i.e., the cosmos) in terms of a holistic vision. It is now nature herself, rather than man, art, or society, that is finally perceived as the absolute form of beauty—"the One differentiated in itself."

Thus we can readily agree with Lawrence Ryan, who sees the novel's conclusion as indicating Hyperion's final realization of his poetic task as urged by Diotima: the priesthood of the divinity of nature.[17] This poetic commitment provides a key to the enigmatic "more later" that concludes the novel. The narrator, who has finally brought his narration to the point where he has become fully at one with his protagonist, promises his friend further correspondence. And yet, strictly considered, he has no more autobiographical information to impart; for, just as the final letter of the novel recounts Hyperion's last experience in Germany immediately preceding his return to Greece, so the first letter had recounted experiences immediately after the return. The letters could not remain retrospective without becoming repetitious. The most plausible interpretation, then, is that the narrator now intends to relate ideas and experiences as they occur—to forward an epistolary diary. And yet the novel concludes; Hyperion ceases to exist as a persona for the author. For, as Ryan argues, in the process of the novel both the narrator Hyperion and the author Hölderlin presumably have arrived at a full awareness of the poetic vocation for which each is suited. *Hyperion* was Hölderlin's first major prose narrative, and it was to be his last. Henceforth his literary productions would predominantly be—after the necessary digression into the dramatic mode in *Empedokles*—elegiac, odic, or hymnic.

Finally, if we accept the interpretation that the narrator matures and develops through the process of recounting his past, we would need to demonstrate that the position expressed at the end of the novel is substantially different from, and superior to, that expressed in the letters at the beginning. We recall that in the first letter the narrator expresses nearly total regret over his past life and bitterly mourns the death of his beloved. The final letter expresses acceptance of all life and the belief that all human separation is ultimately overcome through union in the life of nature.

Nature herself in the early letters is represented as "unchanging"; in the final letter it is viewed as being in constant flux. In the early letters, nature is often addressed as if it were another individual who might console man with her love; in the final letter, such anthropomorphism is not present. It is addressed as a totality in which all individuals are included. In the early letters, Hyperion experiences a state of oblivion in his union with nature; all ordinary modes of understanding are eradicated and all other human experiences are forgotten. Through the vision recorded in the final letter, however, his conscious understanding is enhanced and the totality of experience is reordered and accorded a new, deeper meaning as participating in all-unifying divine life. Finally, and perhaps most significantly, in the early letters, a moment of reflective self-awareness is enough to destroy the pantheistic trance. In the final letter, a pantheistic vision of the universe is strengthened and clarified by reflection, preserved rather than annulled. In the early statement, Hyperion seeks union with the cosmos in subjective, emotional intensity and is cast down after a partial gratification of this subjective quest. In the final statement, he comes to understand himself, objectively, as united with the totality of the cosmos and an integral part of an immortal and unending process.

It is, of course, true that the original experience recounted in the final letter occurred before the experiences recounted in the opening letters. Yet, if we concede that it is here presented as reconstructed by the narrator, we must agree with those critics who argue that the concluding letter, because of the greater maturity and viability of its ideas, indicates that the narrator has achieved a higher level of wisdom and metaphysical sophistication than was evidenced in the earlier letters of the novel.

Chapter Four
"Der Tod des Empedokles"

Hölderlin had long considered classical tragedy the ultimate form of literature. He had contemplated writing a tragedy on a philosophical topic and had once considered a drama on the death of Socrates, using as source probably Plato's *Apology*. By 1797, however, while still living in Frankfurt, he had decided to write a tragedy on the philosopher Empedocles, to whom he had devoted one of his odes.[1]

Hölderlin had probably learned of Empedocles through a third-century (A.D.) treatise by Diogenes Laertius, *The Lives and Opinions of Eminent Philosophers.* It is there stated that Empedocles lived in the Greek colony of Agrigentum, Sicily, in the fifth century B.C. A Pythagorean who later developed his own doctrines, he was a skilled physician reputed to have been a powerful magician able to control the forces of nature. Many people considered him to have divine powers, and Laertius reports that Empedocles had actually asserted his own divinity. Politically, he believed in democracy and at one point refused the offer of a kingship. Philosophically, he believed that the four elements (earth, air, fire, and water) were divine powers and that there was an unending conflict in the universe between the principle of strife, which tended to drive these elements apart, and the principle of love, which sought to bring them together. Empedocles was generally thought to have committed suicide by jumping into the crater of Mount Etna, the Sicilian volcano.[2]

It is easy to understand why this subject might interest the author of *Hyperion.* Like the protagonist of the novel, the historical Empedocles was an extreme idealist both in philosophy and in political theory. Like Hyperion, he was a pantheist, believing in the divinity of nature and of the elements; he was even thought to have such rapport with the elemental powers as to influence them. Consciousness of such power might well have led to overweening pride, or "hubris," an attitude fatal to the protagonists in ancient tragedies. Also, Empedocles' radical political teachings could have brought him into conflict with established society, as was the case with the young Hyperion. Finally, Empedocles' legendary death seemed a nearly perfect instance of self-destructive fusion with the fatally intense divine life of nature. The desire for such a fusion might well occur as a temptation to an enthusiastically devout pantheist.

Hölderlin's initial ideas on the treatment of the topic appeared in the notes known as the "Frankfurter Plan," written at the Gontard house in the summer of 1797.[3] Of chief interest here is his interpretation of the character of Empedokles (Hölderlin's spelling). Hölderlin sees Empedokles as being "disposed to cultural hatred, to contempt for all specific activity, all interest directed at diverse objects"; he hates living in a civilization that compels one to perform special tasks and attend to a multiplicity of trivial details, for such activity leads one into a specialized one-sided existence, the kind of fragmentation for which Hyperion had castigated the Germans. Empedokles is therefore "dissatisfied, restless, miserable even in really beautiful circumstances, merely because they are specific circumstances" and because he would experience human fulfillment only if he could feel a "great accord with all living things." He hates specificity as such because it prevents one from experiencing the totality of life. He is unhappy, finally, because he cannot live and love in the world "with all-present heart, intensely, like a god."

The play itself exists in three versions written chiefly in Homburg during 1798 and 1799. All of them are unfinished, and the first version, although itself fragmentary, is the longest of the three. The first two scenes of act 1 of this version provide the exposition. Laertius had recounted how, among other feats, Empedokles had miraculously cured a dying girl named Panthea, who in Hölderlin's first version is the daughter of Kritias, "archon," or ruler of Agrigentum. In the first scene, Panthea tells her friend Delia that Empedokles, despite his power over nature and his exalted position as messianic leader of the people, has retired to his own garden and seems to be deeply troubled. The following scene permits us to view Empedokles from the opposite perspective—that of his enemies: Kritias, the Archon, representative of the political establishment, and Hermokrates, the priest, representing its religious counterpart. Both feel threatened by Empedokles' radical teachings. Kritias remarks that Empedokles has infected the people with his own spiritual frenzy, so that laws and customs are now generally ignored. The priest, however, declares that the time of Empedokles' influence is at an end. The gods, who once loved him, have now cast him into darkness because, in the intensity of his joy at their intimacy, he "too much forgot the difference" between himself and them. Empedokles is still potentially dangerous, for he might now decide to become a fanatical revolutionary leader bent on the destruction of "law," "art," "custom," and the authority of "holy legend." However, Hermokrates has a plan to take the populace, who believe that Empedokles ascended into heaven, to his garden and show them the philosopher in his present despair and powerlessness. He will then formally lay a curse on Empedokles and urge the people to expel him into the wilderness.

In the third scene, Empedokles appears for the first time and in a soliloquy presents his own version of his fall from grace. He recalls how formerly the divine "forces of life" from the "depths of the world" had all flowed together within himself, so that spiritually "thirsting" men had come to him and found refreshment. Yet, ignoring the fact that the gods had conferred their benefits purely out of love for him, he had believed that he was their master. He fully acknowledges the justice of their punishment and feels that he deserves an even greater debasement. He is unaware that Hermokrates is about to arrange precisely that.

Empedokles is then visited by his pupil, Pausanias.[4] Empedokles explains that he is being punished for having "boasted that he was more than mortal because benevolent Nature had made him too happy." Pausanias asks how the fall from such grace could have happened, and Empedokles reluctantly explains. The nobly simple and "ever youthful" gods of nature had done his bidding, but he had ceased to honor their souls. Instead of supplicating their aid, he conjured them to obey his commands. He thus lost respect for the holiness of Nature:

> Das Leben der Natur, wie sollt' es mir
> Noch heilig sein, wie einst! Die Götter waren
> Mir dienstbar nun geworden, ich allein
> War Gott, und sprachs im frechen Stolz heraus. (4:21)

(The life of Nature, how should it still be holy to me as before! The gods had become serviceable to me, I alone was god and proclaimed it in insolent pride.)

In the following scene, Hermokrates, Kritias, and a number of townspeople intrude into Empedokles' garden. Empedokles prays to be left alone to suffer and die in peace. The people are dumbfounded to hear such talk from a man they had previously deemed divine, and Hermokrates pronounces a curse upon Empedokles and upon anyone who would henceforth associate with him. The superstitious citizens insist upon

Empedokles' immediate departure. Pausanias, of course, defies the curse and declares that he will accompany his master into exile.

The remaining scenes of the first act serve primarily to advance the plot. Empedokles regrets that he has hesitated until such an unseemly moment "to depart"—an ambiguous statement that perhaps already hints at a decision to kill himself. He frees his household slaves, bids farewell to his house and beloved garden, and more clearly reveals his resolve to seek the "quickest" path to the gods. Immediately following his departure, Panthea and Delia come to his house. They find it empty, and Panthea is disconsolate. Delia persuades her to appeal to her father in his behalf.

As the second act opens, Empedokles and Pausanias, already a considerable distance from Agrigentum, are on the slopes of Mount Etna. Unaware of Empedokles' suicidal resolve, Pausanias is under the impression that he is going to accompany his master to Greece. Empedokles tells Pausanias that he is soon to be reconciled both to gods and to mortals. Pausanias, confused, believes that his master has merely attained a state of sublime indifference. Empedokles manages to disabuse his disciple just as they catch sight of a crowd of people, their former neighbors, ascending the mountain.

The fourth scene of the second act is by far the longest in the play. Hermokrates, speaking for the townspeople, proclaims that they have forgiven Empedokles, who has now sufficiently expiated his guilt. Empedokles responds by castigating the people in general and the priest in particular. After Pausanias tells them of Empedokles' decision to commit suicide, the mob abruptly turns upon Hermokrates and threatens him with death. Empedokles nobly intervenes and declares that he has forgiven the people. They joyously offer to make him king, but Empedokles refuses, announcing that "this is no longer the time of kings" and that the people should be prepared to govern themselves. He also gently refuses to return home with them, but he will now bequeath to them his "holiest" possession, a message whose delivery he had long postponed.

Empedokles' sermon expounds the basic principles of his philosophical, religious, and political beliefs—ideas that Hölderlin himself probably espoused at the time. Empedokles declares that man can rejuvenate himself through a voluntary "purifying death" at the "right time." Although this statement obviously refers to his own intended suicide, it becomes clear that it also refers to the collective self-destructions and rejuvenations of entire nations or civilizations through revolutions entailing radical transformations in the form of political, religious, and social life such as had been urged by many of Hölderlin's contemporaries:

So wagts! was ihr geerbt, was ihr erworben,
Was euch der Väter Mund erzählt, gelehrt,
Gesetz und Brauch, der alten Götter Namen,
Vergesst es kühn, und hebt, wie Neugeborne,
Die Augen auf zur göttlichen Natur. (4:65)

(So dare it! What you have inherited, what you have acquired, what your fathers'
mouths told and taught you, law and custom, the names of the old gods—forget
them boldly and, as if newborn, raise up your eyes to divine Nature.)

He urges the people to let their spirits be enkindled to pantheistic rapture
by the "light of heaven." The divine presences of the natural world would
then be manifest to them all and they would be possessed by the spirit of
peace which is the "life of the world." Full of this deific spirit, they would
construct their "own beautiful world" in human society; they would join
hands in universal brotherhood and love and "divide the good." ("Das
Gut" in the German text could refer either to spiritual blessings or to
material possessions; presumably both are intended here.) They could then
invite the gods themselves, the spirits of ever-changing nature, to an
unending festive celebration.

In response to the crowd's repeated urgings that he return to live with
them, Empedokles declares that the gods themselves had arranged his
public humiliation and ostracism as a sign that "the time of his purification" had come and to warn him lest once again "the friend of the gods"
might become an object of "sport and mockery and scandal" among men.
He needed no second warning, for he realizes now that he had been
essentially a "stranger among them" and born to live only for a short time.
Again, he bids them farewell. If they need human advice, they should
apply to Pausanias. Moreover, the message he has given them is enough for
them to live on; they have no further need of his presence. He must die, as
befits one who has been the instrument of a divine revelation.

In the following scene, Empedokles seeks to console Pausanias. He
explains that he does not wish to outlive the day of his dishonor; there will
always abide an immortal and divine "Spirit of love" between them.
Empedokles then bids him to prepare a last supper of bread and wine that
they may feast and sing together a last "hymn of praise" to the muses. In
a final soliloquy after Pausanias's departure, Empedokles calls upon the
god Jupiter as his liberator. As an evening wind blows upon him, he feels
divine inspiration come over him more intensely than ever before.
Feeling all the joys of "one who overcomes," he seems to himself truly

now to live fully for the first time. He now seeks nothing but his "place of sacrifice."

Two additional fragmentary scenes are associated with the first version. In terms of the action of the play, they are situated after Empedokles' last soliloquy but before his death. They consist, respectively, of a conversation between Panthea and Delia and a conversation between the two women and Pausanias; in these the characters air their opinions on Empedokles' impending suicide.

When we consider Empedokles as he is presented in the first version of the play, perhaps his most obvious characteristic is his similarity to the Christ of the Gospels. Like Christ, he is a religious leader with miraculous powers, able to heal the sick and control natural forces. He presents to his followers, and to people in general, a fresh revelation of the Deity. This arouses the hostility of the traditional priesthood, represented by Hermokrates, who corresponds to the Caiphas of the Gospels. The priest bides his time and, when the moment is right, succeeds in turning most of the people against him on charges of fraud and blasphemy. The civil ruler, Kritias, consents to this condemnation; he corresponds roughly to Pilate. Empedokles is virtually condemned to death; before he dies, however, he appoints a successor, his most trusted disciple. He accepts his death freely, and before dying he intends to celebrate a solemn last supper of bread and wine. If we consider Hölderlin's theological background, we must conclude that such similarities are neither coincidental nor unintentional.

However, Empedokles' points of dissimilarity with Christ in this version are equally significant. Here the people change their minds about condemning him; he triumphs over his priestly foe and resolves to kill himself against the wishes of the people and their civil ruler. Even more important are the essential differences between the religious teachings of Christ and those of Empedokles. According to the traditional interpretation of the Gospels, Christ preaches belief in and worship of an anthropomorphic Father God who is essentially identical with the God of the Old Testament. Moreover, most of Christ's ethical teachings might be considered developments or amplifications of those of the Hebrew scriptures. Empedokles, on the other hand, preaches an impersonal pantheism, the worship of nature as the divine life of the world and of her manifestations in the world's natural phenomena. Although Empedokles sometimes refers to anthropomorphic deities such as Jupiter, it is usually the elemental deities, impersonal in form although seemingly personal in their mode of interaction with him, that Empedokles refers to as his "gods." Empedokles, unlike Christ, is alienated from these gods by an act of hubris, and they abandon him. The primary motive for his suicide is his desire to be reunited to the gods through self-immolation, thereby extinguishing his individual consciousness (which had led him to his sin of pride) and returning the elements of his own body to the totality of nature, his ultimate deity. Christ's death, although likewise freely chosen, had the primary function (according to the traditional Pauline interpretation) of redeeming mankind from its collective debt of sin and thereby restoring man to the good graces of God the Father. There is no indication in the first version of the play that Empedokles expected that his death would benefit other people in any way; he is uninfluenced by their pleas that he continue to guide and assist them in their lives. There appears to be no altruism in his decision to die.

Hölderlin probably abandoned his work on the first version sometime early in 1799 and wrote the scenes that are said to constitute the second version in the early summer of that year. It has been noted that he apparently intended to shorten the play by omitting many of the less essential scenes.[5] Thus, the introductory first scene of act 1 is omitted. A revised version of the initial conversation between the priest and the archon (renamed Mekades) here constitutes the opening scene, while a revision of Empedokles' first soliloquy becomes scene 2. The third scene of this version, accordingly, corresponds to the fourth scene. There remain two fragmentary scenes, judged by Beissner to be meant for the concluding section of the second act, which are expansions of the sketchy later scenes of the first version.[6] Although it appears that no more was written, it may be assumed that Hölderlin still intended to complete the play in five acts. The extant second version of the drama is thus more fragmentary than the first.

The general conception of the plot and of the character of Empedokles remains basically unchanged. A significant difference in form is the poet's use of a different metrical pattern. The verse of the first version had been fairly conventional blank verse, with only conventional variations. Here, however, while leaving large sections in the original meter, Hölderlin frequently employs a kind of free verse with a variable number of feet per line. Critics have pointed out that this verse form allows the poet greater concision and force of expression and anticipates the unusual metrical patterns of the later hymns.[7] Other differences between the versions include changes of emphasis in characterizations and in the ideas expressed by the protagonist.

The most significant deviations from the first version occur in the first scene, the conversation between Hermokrates and the archon. Although now renamed Mekades, the archon is basically the same person as the Kritias of the first version and says most of the same things, the only difference being that Mekades appears to be somewhat younger and more naive. The character of Hermokrates, however, has been drastically altered. In the first version, he was presented as a malevolent bigot who feared and hated Empedokles as a threat to his own priestly power over the masses. Here, he is a man of considerable wisdom, even compassion, who understands Empedokles fairly well, has some sympathy for him, and offers his own sophisticated analysis of Empedokles' fall from the gods' favor. His main reason for disapproving of Empedokles is that Empedokles was sacrilegiously indiscreet in revealing his knowledge of divine mysteries to the common people. Because of this fatal error, he fully deserves his fate, and Hermokrates, although sympathetic toward him, feels morally justified in helping to bring about his downfall and humiliation.

The second scene, Empedokles' monologue, is not significantly different from the equivalent scene in the first version, but there is some change in the protagonist's account of the sin that caused his fall from grace. While in the first version the account was analytical, it is here allegorical. The gods had offered him the sacred nectar of their grace and he had imbibed too deeply, becoming so mightily "drunk" that he derided them. As before, the monologue ends ironically with Empedokles' plea for someone to avenge his crimes.

The third (fragmentary) scene between Empedokles and Pausanias has been thoroughly rewritten, although the basic characterizations and the intellectual content are unchanged. This scene is now better organized and the rhetoric of the speeches is clearer and more concise. A notable difference in strategy is seen in the fact that Pausanias, who in the first version immediately perceives Empedokles' fallen condition and repeatedly urges him to reclaim his powers, here believes that his master is still in possession of his former faculties. Empedokles therefore seeks to convince him that his fall was real.

The two remaining scenes in this version consist of conversations between Panthea, Delia, and Pausanias. These scenes are of interest because they show, for the first time, someone seriously questioning the moral rectitude of Empedokles' intended suicide. In the first, Panthea is expressing sympathy for Empedokles and approval of his suicidal decision, but Delia objects to her approbation. In the second, Pausanias appears and

asks the women if they know of Empedokles' whereabouts; he declares that
Empedokles alone is destined to undertake "with glory" a suicide that no
one else could commit without a "curse." He is wholly convinced of the
justness of his master's decision. Delia objects that Empedokles is sacrific-
ing himself "too gladly," but Panthea proclaims that the nobility of his
departure fills her with "holy joy." Moreover, his sacrifice is necessary:

> So will es der Geist
> Und die reifende Zeit,
> Denn Einmal bedurften
> Wir Blinden des Wunders. (4:118)

(The Spirit and ripening Time will it thus, for we blind ones once had need of a
miracle.)

Panthea's declaration, which concludes this version, is obscure and
mysterious; it raises for the first time the issue of the historical significance
of Empedokles' death, which is seen as inevitable, even divinely ordained,
and for some reason necessary as a revelation to others.

Hölderlin abandoned work on the second version sometime in the
summer of 1799 and began to work on a third presumably in September.
Whereas the second version was merely a revision of the first, the completed portions of the third version show it to be a radically different play.
The issue of Empedokles' fall from grace is now deemphasized, and the
problematical character of his death becomes of central importance. Emphasis is placed on the question of the moral validity of his suicide and on
the problem of its spiritual effect upon the people of his country.[8] The
conception of Empedokles' character is accordingly altered to make him, if
possible, even more grandiose and now fully conscious of the historical
significance and efficacy of his death. His religious and political opposition
is combined into one person, Strato, the king of Agrigent and Empedokles' own brother—thus making the conflict even more intense. This
version also introduces a major new character, Manes, Empedokles' old
teacher, who directly challenges the rectitude of his pupil's suicidal intent
and forces him to defend it. From the three extant scenes and from
Hölderlin's detailed outline for the completion of the play, we can also see a
new conception of the plot in accordance with the general shift of emphasis. In this version, the action begins on Mount Etna after Empedokles
has been expelled from town. The exposition of the preceding events
occurs in an opening monologue and is extremely brief in comparison with

the previous versions. The second scene, corresponding to the fifth scene of act 2 of the first version, is a conversation between Empedokles and Pausanias. The third and last completed scene is the confrontation between Empedokles and Manes. According to Hölderlin's outline, there were to have been several additional scenes in the first act and four additional acts. Most of the subsequent action of the play would have been devoted to the process whereby Empedokles becomes reconciled to the other characters and whereby they come to a complete understanding of the full significance of his death. In this version, also, Hölderlin returns to the use of blank verse. Perhaps he felt that the freer metrics of the second version were unsuitable for classical drama, or that they provided insufficient artistic discipline; at any event, the verse in this play is extremely taut and dense in texture and as poetry is generally superior to the verse of the previous versions.

Before writing the third version, however, Hölderlin wrote a speculative piece of prose, the "Grund zum Empedokles," in which he theorizes about the problems of the drama, particularly the justification and historical impact of Empedokles' life and death.[9] He writes that there is operative within both individual and society a dialectical conflict between two opposing principles which he terms the *organisch* and the *aorgisch*. The *organisch* is the principle of rational organization; it refers to all modes of order consciously devised or imposed by man. The *aorgisch*, on the other hand, refers to everything that is beyond the scope or control of human consciousness: the forces of nature, the unconscious and irrational within man or society, and any manifestation of divine being or power. Empedokles' Agrigentum is a land where the forces of the *organisch* and the *aorgisch* are in violent opposition: its citizens (like modern Europeans) are overly rationalistic and irreverent in their thinking and behavior. Without respecting the forces of nature, they seek technological mastery over them; yet they often give way to violent outbursts of the irrational within themselves. Empedokles shows them the error of their ways, both demonstrating and verbally articulating the divinity of nature, thus achieving within himself a reconciliation between the *aorgisch* (divine nature) and the *organisch* (consciousness and language). But this synthesis is at first achieved only within Empedokles. The people will never achieve his degree of spiritual harmony and enlightenment as long as he is present, for they are content passively to listen to his wisdom. Thus, Hölderlin argues, Empedokles must die if his enlightenment is to be achieved by others, leading to the spiritual rejuvenation of society. Empedokles' own personal (and temporary) fall from grace is thus now considered less a matter of personal guilt than of historical necessity. It was necessary for him to experience an "excess of intensity" ("Übermass der Innigkeit") in thinking himself equal to the gods, and subsequently to fall, if he is to be moved to die and to understand his self-inflicted death as a prerequisite for the "release" of his "spirit" upon the people. These ideas, worked out in the abstruse prose of the essay, are given their poetic expression in the third scene of this version of the play. It is, of course, possible to see in them another point of comparison between Empedokles and Christ: Christ also had to die before his spirit could be released at Pentecost, leading ultimately to the establishment of a church and civilization allegedly inspired by him.

The third scene commences with an abrupt confrontation between Empedokles and his old teacher. Manes, who has heard of his decision, warns him that he will not escape the "wrath of heaven" if he commits suicide. He then proclaims the one instance in which a religious suicide would be admissible: it must be performed by precisely the right person at the right time. Like a "grapevine," such a man would be the child both of earthly darkness and of heavenly light, thus combining in himself divine and human attributes. His world must be one of political and religious ferment, where old beliefs and institutions are being challenged and overthrown (as in Hölderlin's Europe); in terms of the "Grund," there must be drastic conflict between the *organisch* and the *aorgisch*. The divine ruler of the historical process, angered at the prospect of losing control, dispatches furious "lightning-bolts" of heavenly wrath; yet such manifestations merely exacerbate the conflict. At this moment of extreme crisis, there is need of a man who could reconcile the divine and human elements within himself so that the objective "conflict of the world" becomes subjectively "mild" in him. By his example, he could then disseminate peace and harmony, reconciling "men" and "gods." Yet, to prevent this virtual demigod from being idolized as greater than the gods themselves and to allow the "holy Spirit of Life" which he possesses to be released into the souls of others, it is (as argued in the "Grund") necessary for him to die. And it is best that death be accomplished "purely" in holy self-sacrifice.

Manes then challenges Empedokles on his qualifications for being the "new savior." In response, Empedokles retells the story of his life, effectively demonstrating that he does qualify and paraphrasing much that was said about him in the "Grund." In this speech, nothing is said about hubris, and there is only a fleeting reference to past suffering. Empedokles' account of his early personal harmony with the gods is here marked by an emphasis on how he could articulate the essences of these otherwise alien elemental deities when he "named with names the gods of nature," thus bringing the *aorgisch* forces into the *organisch* realm of language: he "solved the riddle of life" in "word" and in "image." Yet he could not repose in this subjective accomplishment because of the tumultuous unrest in his world, the drastic conflict within his countrymen between rationalistic nihilism and primitive passions. Confronted with this situation, Empedokles suddenly realized that the presiding deity of his nation was abandoning it: "Es war der scheidende Gott meines Volks" (4:137). The spiritual consensus that had maintained the order of this civilization was itself a divine power in the process of disappearing. Empedokles felt it his duty to "reconcile" this deity with his countrymen much as Christ had attempted at first to establish a more vital relationship between his people and their God. And he succeeded, for the people were pacified and once more enjoyed intimacy with their "living gods." Yet, despite his people's gratitude, Empedokles realized that he was destined for a sacrifical death:

> Denn wo ein Land ersterben soll, da wählt
> Der Geist noch Einen sich zuletzt, durch den
> Sein Schwanensang, das letzte Leben tönet.
> Wohl ahndet ichs, doch dient' ich willig ihm.
> Es ist geschehen. (4:138)

(For when a country is to die, the Spirit chooses one more man for itself at last, through whom its swan song, the last life, resounds. Indeed I suspected this, yet I served it willingly. It has happened.)

He will soon be joined to the elemental gods and "in death find . . . the Living." He predicts that to celebrate his death there will occur simultaneously an eruption of Etna and a violent thunderstorm, envisioned as an orgiastic reunion of the gods Sky and Earth. Empedokles confidently declares that he is ending his days "in free death according to divine law." Manes remains skeptical as the scene ends.

In the outline or plan of the third version, appended to the "Grund," Hölderlin wrote a series of cryptic notes, often consisting of single words, indicating how this version of the play was to be completed.[10] There were to be several more scenes in the first act. The next would introduce Empedokles' chief opponent in this version, his royal brother Strato, who in a lengthy note is described as reconsidering his expulsion of Empedokles from Agrigentum. He decides to revoke his order not only because the people are already regretting the loss of their prophet but also because of a "secret bond" between himself and Empedokles. A complete reconciliation eventually takes place. Notes for the remaining five acts of the play are extremely sketchy. It seems that Empedokles was to have appeared for the last time at the end of act 4 and that his suicide was to have occurred before the end of the play. An important concluding note for the fifth act indicates that Manes is finally convinced that Empedokles is indeed the historical redeemer he claimed to be. He declares that Empedokles is "the chosen one who kills and gives life, in and through whom a world is at once dissolved and renewed." Empedokles totally understood the nature of his land's "perishing" and so was able fully to anticipate the form of its "new life." Thus, Manes announces, he "intends to proclaim to them what the last will of Empedokles was," for this would be the document on which the new civilization would be based.

The various versions of the Empedokles drama show an important development in Hölderlin's thinking. In the earliest plan, Empedokles was seen principally as a poet-prophet without honor in his own country—rather as Hölderlin himself must have felt during the last phase of his employment at the Gontard house. In the first two extant versions of the play, emphasis is placed on Empedokles' hubris or guilt—seen variously as a result of contempt for the gods or as a consequence of his having betrayed his secrets to the uninitiated. The second version shows greater respect for the conservative religious philosophy of Hermokrates, indicating a tendency that will become more pronounced in Hölderlin's last hymns. In both versions, death is sought for a personal reason, a desire to merge with the gods. Hölderlin rethought the problems of the play in the "Grund zum Empedokles," and in the third version the emphasis is almost wholly on the historical significance of Empedokles' death. The development here is summarized, as critics have observed, in a cryptic note in the outline of the third version, marking a "transition from the subjective to the objective."[11] Instead of dwelling on his personal, subjective problems (Hölderlin had decided), a poet should, like the later Empedokles, devote himself to proclaiming an objective, universal vision: nothing less than the anticipated return of the vanished gods and the establishment of an ideally harmonious new world. The attempt at adequate articulation of this vision was to be the dominant concern of the later poems which—most critics feel—represent Hölderlin's greatest poetic achievement. Hölderlin thus abandons the dramatic mode (and the play itself) for the elegiac and hymnic forms in which his vision could be more directly and forcefully proclaimed.

Chapter Five
The Odes

In an earlier chapter we noted how, in his adolescence, Hölderlin had composed a number of odes in imitation of Klopstock. About 1797, however, he began experimentally to adapt ancient Greek ode forms, the Alcaic and the Asclepidean, into quantitative German verse. The two forms have much in common: the basic unit of each is a four-line stanza consisting of two longer lines, with caesuras, followed by two shorter lines; both employ traditional classical meter, with iambs and dactyls predominating. The difference, it has been noted, is that the Alcaic ode is distinguished by smoother meters and easier transitions than are found in the more abrupt Asclepidean ode, where pauses are more heavily stressed.[1] Hölderlin thus was inclined to use the Alcaic form when seeking a smooth development of images and ideas, as when a narrative element is dominant; he tended to employ the other form for those poems in which he desired to stress antithetical oppositions between ideas or images.

Hölderlin's earliest odes in these meters are brief, even epigrammatic. He explicitly justifies this quality in the antithetical rhythms of an Asclepidian ode, "Die Kürze" ("Brevity"):

> "Warum bist du so kurz? liebst du, wie vormals, denn
> Nun nicht mehr den Gesang? fandst du, als Jüngling, doch,
>   In den Tagen der Hoffnung,
>   Wenn du sangest, das Ende nie!" (1:248)

("Why are you so brief? Do you no longer love song, as before? Indeed, as a youth, in the days of hope, you never found the end when you sang.")

The response, already anticipated in the question, is that song is commensurate with happiness: true inspiration is compatible only with joyous peace of mind, which the poet now lacks. It must be recalled that at the probable time of the poem's composition (1798) Hölderlin was generally unhappy in his personal life. A number of odes thus reflect his now deeply troubled relationship with "Diotima." In an eight-line Alcaic ode addressed to her, the poet offers her reassurance. He grants that she is misunderstood by present-day "barbarians"; she longs for the society of refined and "tenderly magnanimous" souls like her own. Yet the day is coming when the world will be raised to her own spiritual level. Another group of brief odes written at this time are concerned with poetic problems. In the Alcaic ode "An die Parzen" (addressed to the fates who control men's lives), the poet poignantly calls out:

> Nur Einen Sommer gönnt, ihr Gewaltigen!
> Und einen Herbst zu reifem Gesange mir,
>   Dass williger mein Herz, vom süssen
>   Spiele gesättiget, dann mir sterbe. (1:241)

(Only one summer grant me, you mighty ones! And an autumn for ripe song, so that more willingly my heart might then die for me, sated with sweet play.)

To achieve the perfect "poem" (possibly meaning the completed Empedokles tragedy) would be enough to justify the speaker's hitherto failed existence. Its accomplishment would give him a moment of god-like joy and fulfillment, after which death would be a matter of indifference. Although "An die Parzen" is perhaps Hölderlin's most widely admired ode of this period, the first ode to make a major poetic statement is "Der Mensch," probably written in 1798. He here views man and his relation to the world from a perspective radically different from that attained at the close of *Hyperion,* where the narrator sees mankind as passively acquiescent. Man is presented as engaged in an unending, almost Faustian striving for totality. Critics have noted that the ode thus represents somewhat of a return to the Fichtean position Hölderlin had earlier (if tentatively) espoused.

   A number of odes which were written about the turn of the century are all concerned in some way with the poet's fatherland. Two of these, "Der Main" and "Der Neckar," named after two rivers familiar to Hölderlin, meditatively contrast idyllic German scenes with those of the poet's ideal homeland, Greece. "Heidelberg," one of Hölderlin's most beloved poems, likewise celebrates a specific German site, but is atypical of Hölderlin's poetry in that it actually evokes the spirit of a place rather than merely situating the place within the general context of a symbolic

geography. It is also one of his most precisely descriptive poems, for
most of his poetry is dominated by ideas and narration rather than
description. After an initial stanza of general praise for the beauty of the
city, the poem describes in loving detail the bridge, the river (the
Neckar), the ancient castle seemingly rejuvenated by sunlight and living
ivy, the hillsides, the banks, and the pleasant lanes and gardens of the
city.

> Aber schwer in das Tal hing die gigantische,
>   Schicksalskundige Burg nieder bis auf den Grund,
>   Von den Wettern zerrissen;
>   Doch die ewige Sonne goss
>
> Ihr verjüngendes Licht über das alternde
>   Riesenbild, und umher grünte lebendiger
>   Efeu; freundliche Wälder
>   Rauschten über die Burg herab.
>
> Sträuche blühten herab, bis wo im heitern Tal,
>   An den Hügel gelehnt, oder dem Ufer hold,
>   Deine fröhlichen Gassen
>   Unter duftenden Gärten ruhn. (14–15:21–32)

(But the gigantic, fate-announcing fortress, torn by storms, inclined heavily
down into the base of the valley; yet the eternal sun poured her rejuvenating
light over the aging giant image, and living ivy was greening all around,
friendly forests rustled down over the fortress. Shrubs were blossoming [all the
way] down to where in the cheerful valley, leaning upon the hill or the splendid
banks, your friendly lanes repose amidst fragrant gardens.)

    Two closely related odes celebrate Hölderlin's return to his native
province of Swabia after his prolonged absence in Frankfurt and Homburg. In "Die Heimat," the gloomier of the two, he looks forward to his
return but doubts that the joys of home can heal the sufferings of his
frustrated love for Susette. The poem concludes with a philosophical
statement, echoing a passage in *Hyperion,* to the effect that "holy
suffering" is given to us by the gods and needs to be accepted in
resignation. Greater consolation is offered by the companion ode,
"Rückkehr in die Heimat," a song of exuberant praise addressed to his
native province. The poet's suffering is here (as in the later hymn "Der
Rhein") viewed as a testing process whereby the excessive desires of

youth are tempered and reduced to a mature silence in the face of destiny. In the final stanza he anticipates a new, settled existence.

We know, of course, that Hölderlin's life was never to remain settled for long until his final madness. The political agitations of the turn of the century, the French wars in which the German states were involved, and the concomitant conspiracies (encouraged by the general turmoil) for democratic revolutions in Germany prompted Hölderlin to write two of his most overtly political poems since the Tübingen hymns. For the past several years, the divine entities celebrated in his poetry and his novel had almost exclusively been nature (the pantheistic divine life of the world) and her principal elements. In the ode "Der Zeitgeist," however, a new deity is hailed, one that will play an increasingly important role in Hölderlin's later poetry: the "god of time," the director and motivating force of historical process. In this poem, he is also the "time-spirit," the animated prevailing idea of a given moment, impelling groups of historically attuned individuals to action when the time is right. The poem's conclusion concedes that political participation can lead some to evil, but only "bad" men become worse and meet a quicker end when seized upon by this god.[2]

Where such commitment to political action might have led the poet is evidenced by one of his most bizarre poems, "Der Tod fürs Vaterland." Not since the Tübingen hymns had revolutionary zeal been so evidently expressed, and in perhaps no other poem by Hölderlin is violence so evidently relished. Moreover, there is a nationalistic component in the poem's enthusiasm that has subjected it to gross misinterpretations by chauvinistic German readers. It must be kept in mind, however, that the political mood here remains primarily revolutionary in intent. The "fatherland" so zealously evoked is a country that is drastically to be transfigured into an ideal democracy; the enemy, addressed as "murderers," are almost certainly the forces of German feudal tyranny attempting to suppress the rebellion. The poem envisions a future battle in which revolutionary forces will triumph. One need not "count the dead" after this battle, for "not one too many" could have fallen for such a cause.

Hölderlin's patriotism is given a more appealing (if equally nationalistic) form of expression in "Gesang des Deutschen," the longest and most ambitious ode he had yet written. An Alcaic ode of fifteen stanzas, it proclaims a vision of a spiritually transfigured Germany that would rival the intellectual and cultural achievements of ancient Greece and assume spiritual leadership of the world. Here, for the first time in his mature work, Hölderlin announces that his own country is capable of such transfiguration, expressing the same hopes for Germany that Hyperion in the novel had held for Greece. The poet hails Germany, the poet's fatherland, as "holy heart of the nations"—alluding both to Germany's central geographical position in Europe and to her ideal role as spiritual center:

> Du Land des hohen ernsteren Genius!
> Du Land der Liebe! bin ich der deine schon,
>   Oft zürnt' ich weinend, dass du immer
>   Blöde die eigene Seele leugnest. (3:10–15)

(You land of high, more serious Genius! You land of love! I am already yours [and] I have often wept in rage that you always foolishly deny your own soul.)

Hölderlin then propounds a view of history implicit in several of his later works: "Genius," the godlike creative spirit (and, concomitantly, the spiritual leadership of the world), resides in different national cultures at different historical periods; it "wanders like the Spring from land to land."[3] Originally situated in Asia, it moved to Greece and subsequently to Rome; it is now to emerge again in full flower in modern Europe, particularly in Germany, which will soon achieve intellectual and spiritual prominence among her neighbors. Germany, like ancient Greece, thus has the capability not only to attain national unity but also to achieve a cultural coherence through which daily life will be experienced as an unending feast.

Two closely related odes, "An die Deutschen" and "Rousseau," develop further this theme of anticipation of a cultural utopia. Both are incomplete; from the manuscript it is not clear whether Hölderlin intended to complete the former poem or merely abandoned it for the likewise unfinished "Rousseau." The first section of "An die Deutschen" urges the poet's countrymen not to mock at a child astride a rocking-horse, for "we too are poor in deeds and full of thoughts"—meaning that the Germans are now speculative thinkers who seem unlikely to translate their plans into action. Yet, the poet confesses, such speculation may indeed result in deeds, as clouds produce lightning. The present "silence" among his countrymen might be the awe preceding the great feast foreseen in "Gesang des Deutschen" and the concomitant arrival of a god, whereupon German mountains would, like Parnassus in Greece, become "mountains of the muses," abodes of divine sources of inspiration, and everywhere beneath the golden heaven of the fatherland "free, clear, spiritual joy" would glisten.[4] In the last completed section of the ode, the poet turns to his own predicament as visionary prophet. Although sure of the authenticity of his vision, he is anxious about when and how the vision will ever become reality. His longing for its future realization often estranges him from the present, so that his soul yearns longingly beyond his own time while he stands desolately on its cold shores, alienated and yet unable to perceive the "promised" ones of a future generation ultimately more akin to himself. He now fears that he might sink down into oblivion "without name and unmourned."

"Rousseau" is basically a revision and extension of the concluding section of the previous poem. Its first line, "Wie eng begrenzt ist unsere Tageszeit," is closely parallel to the first line of the eleventh stanza of the other ("Wohl ist enge begrenzt unsere Lebenszeit") and sets the theme of the entire poem, in which the role of the lonely prophet is transferred from Hölderlin to Rousseau. Although Rousseau has been dead for many years and although the French Revolution was largely fought in his name, he still remains a shadowy figure to his uncomprehending fellow-Europeans.[5] Like Hölderlin, he yet stands waiting disconsolately on the present shore for the promised godlike people of the utopian future, whom he could greet as true friends and who would correctly interpret his "lonely discourse." The remainder of this fragmentary poem, then, is an attempt to console the shade of Rousseau and, implicitly, the poet himself.

At this time, when a historical vision was taking shape in his poetry, Hölderlin returned in some of his odes to the topic of his personal experience, particularly his continuing frustrated love for "Diotima." Some of these poems are expansions of epigrams or short odes written several years earlier: "Die Liebe," "Diotima," and "Der Abschied." Perhaps the most extensive expansion occurs in "Der Abschied," where one stanza is developed into ten. The original poem had proclaimed that the particular "god" of love prevailing between himself and Diotima had been "murdered" at their forced separation. In the present poem, Hölderlin states that he himself had been incapable of killing the "animating, protecting god" of their love. It had been slain rather by the selfish spirit of worldliness (i.e., the animus possessing Gontard and his friends), the force of hideous "fear" or anxiety that has ever demanded to be appeased by the sacrifice of lovers' hearts.

"Natur und Kunst, oder Saturn und Jupiter" is one of Hölderlin's best-known odes and perhaps one of the most intrinsically difficult. In it, the poet returns to serious allegory for the first time since his unsuccessful experiments with the mode in the Tübingen hymns. Saturn here represents "nature" and Jupiter personifies "art." It has been observed that in this poem, as elsewhere in Hölderlin's works, "Nature" means the divine soul or life force of the universe, a shaping power that is itself amorphous.[6] "Art" here means human consciousness and whatever has been shaped or ordered by it—modes of thought and all products of thought, even the very structures of civilization. "Nature" and "art" thus correspond respectively to the Empedoklean concepts of *"aorgisch"* and *"organisch."* Jupiter not only represents such rational mental activities but also, as the rational principle personified, he has been symbolic ruler of the world ever since man first achieved consciousness and began imposing order on existence. Saturn, on the other hand (who, according to myth, was Jupiter's father, eventually deposed and imprisoned in the underworld by his rebellious son), was the god of the legendary "golden age" of human innocence corresponding to the state of childhood in the individual. Life under Saturn thus had the dreamlike indeterminacy of the "Einfalt" described in the preface to *Hyperion,* a condition abandoned as soon as man began to think.

In the first stanza, Jupiter ("Saturn's son") is hailed as reigning high in the daytime sky like the sun at noon; his law flourishes, he holds the scales of justice, gives men their allotments, and "rests happily in the fame of his immortal arts of ruling." All these attributes are traditional in classical literature. However, if we interpret Jupiter here as "art" or rational ordering activity, we may infer that such rationality has reached its zenith in the eighteenth century, especially in the philosophies of Kant and Fichte.[7] The "law" is the principle of rational order; the scales and allotments signify the judgmental function stressed by Kant. At this point, rationality seems confident and secure. In the second and third stanzas, the poet charges (again in keeping with tradition) that Jupiter banished his holy father to the "abyss," the Tartarean underworld. When man first achieved rational consciousness, the principle of intuitive, preconscious life was repressed or banished to neglect. The fourth and fifth stanzas comprise the poet's demand on Jupiter and their justification. The god is ordered either to descend from his position or not to be ashamed of gratitude toward his father. If he wishes to remain in power he must serve the elder god and allow poets to celebrate Saturn above all other beings. Thus, "art," or rationality, is ordered either to abdicate (an alternative presented for rhetorical purposes) or to acknowledge the preeminence of "nature," or intuitively harmonious life, in regulating human existence.

In the final two stanzas, the poet turns to his own experiences and relates them to the major theme of the poem. He declares that his own final recognition of the character and power of Jupiter depends on three conditions:

> Und hab' ich erst am Herzen Lebendiges
> Gefühlt und dämmert, was du gestaltetest,
> Und war in ihrer Wiege mir in
> Wonne die wechselnde Zeit entschlummert:
>
> Dann kenn ich dich, Kronion! dann hör ich dich,
> Den weisen Meister, welcher, wie wir, ein Sohn
> Der Zeit, Gesetze gibt und, was die
> Heilige Dämmerung birgt, verkündet. (2:37–38)

(. . . and once I have felt the Living in my heart and [once] that which you have formed has gone into twilight, and if changing time has blissfully fallen asleep for me in her cradle:

Then I will know you, Son of Chronos! then I will hear you, the wise master who, like us a son of time, gives laws and proclaims what the holy twilight conceals.)

These concluding stanzas are extremely difficult to interpret. The crucial concept here appears to be "time." Yet the word *time* is used in two apparently contradictory ways, for it is only after "changing time" has fallen asleep that Jupiter can be hailed as a "son of time." (It was once believed that the Greek word for Saturn, *Kronos*, was related to the word for time, *Chronos*—a confusion that led to the traditional identification of Saturn with Father Time.) One solution to this problem is to posit the presence of two radically different concepts of time: "changing" time and the time represented by Saturn, that of the "Golden Age" (in German, "die goldene *Zeit*"). Changing time is time as we experience it through rational consciousness, time as mutability, whereas Saturnian time is time experienced more as Bergsonian duration, an unbroken and seemingly unvarying continuum. When the changing time of anxious, reflective rationality falls asleep, this is the time to which we will revert—the rational, conceptual structures of Jupiter's world will lapse into the dimness of twilight and seeming irrelevancy and we will momentarily return to peaceful preconsciousness, feeling at one with the all-pervading life of the world. This, then, is why poets are urged to "name" Saturn; this poetic naming is to be an invocation, calling upon him to impart his divine peace. Only after Saturn, the principle of all-unitive nature fully *experienced,* has been fully recognized, can Saturn's paternal role be understood as the ultimate source of our conscious existence as well as of the rational principle (Jupiter) itself. Reason, properly chastened, will then proclaim and fully articulate the meaning of preconscious life, hidden though now it be in "holy twilight" beyond reason's domain. The ending of the poem retains some residual ambiguity, for the "twilight" here may be either an enduring alternative condition, owing to the structure of the psyche with its conscious and nonconscious aspects, or a "Götterdämmerung" for Jupiter/art/reason and a return to the reign of Saturn/nature/unconsciousness. While the latter possibility is not to be excluded, the rhetoric of the last stanza suggests that Jupiter is to be reinstated to a more acceptable dominance.

An ode written perhaps in the same year, "Unter den Alpen gesungen," is possibly the only poem composed by Hölderlin in the form (slightly altered) of the classical Sapphic ode.[8] It was probably written or at least conceived early in 1801 during Hölderlin's residence in Hauptwil, Switzerland. The poem is a hymn in praise of "holy innocence," a condition of complete spiritual simplicity and passive, receptive openness to nature and the divine forces. Such a state is comparable to, if not identical with, the "wise passiveness" advocated by Wordsworth in the *Lyrical Ballads.* It is also characterized by the unreflectiveness associated with Saturn in the previous ode.

"Dichterberuf," written in 1800 or 1801, is often considered to be Hölderlin's greatest ode. In it, he delineates a highly original view of the poet's "calling."[9] As it is one of his most difficult poems, critics seem unable to agree on any one interpretation. The following analysis, then, is merely one possible way of reading the poem. Like several of the later odes, "Dichterberuf" is the expansion of an earlier, shorter poem. The first stanza, borrowed intact from the earlier ode, is one of the most striking passages in Hölderlin's work:

> Des Ganges Ufer hörten des Freudengotts
> Triumph, als allerobernd vom Indus her
> Der junge Bacchus kam, mit heilgem
> Weine vom Schlafe die Völker weckend. (46:1–4)

(The Ganges' banks heard the triumph of the God of Joy, as all-conquering from the Indus young Bacchus approached, awakening the nations from [their] sleep with holy wine.)

Hölderlin here echoes ancient myth in his account of Dionysos's triumphal procession through India, where the god taught various peoples the cultivation of the grape and the subsequent joy of wine drinking; the poet interprets such activity as arousing culturally dormant nations to a spiritual, "holy" joy through awareness of divine presence.[10] The poet then hails the "angel of day," who can be interpreted as the sun in its divine aspect, Apollo, god of the poets. This deity, acting as angelic messenger, is called upon to awaken sleeping peoples today, much as Bacchus had done in ancient times. For poetry, like "holy wine," should elevate men toward a more intensely spiritual perception of divinity, enabling them to perceive and proclaim new divine "laws" (moral, esthetic, or metaphysical) to govern the world. Poets, called upon to be such conquering, life-and-law-giving agents of Apollo, must devote themselves to "The Highest" (presumably not Apollo but the highest God, Father Aether, the transcendent life principle of the universe), and repeatedly sing his praises.

The poet then celebrates the recent arrival of the god of poetry, the "genius" of divine creative inspiration in modern Europe. Apollo is seen as controlling and directing violent historical energies to his own purposes. As sun-god, he is in control of the events of the day. The present genius of poetry is here identical with the historical spirit of the age; in both cases, Apollo uses human agents to accomplish his ultimate designs.[11] The poet declares that he and his fellow poets should not remain silent about such historical manifestations of the creative spirit. He then turns to a polemic against the misuse of poetry springing from a frivolous concept of the duty of poets; many contemporary poets, he declares, have irresponsibly toyed with their genius. As such playfulness carried to the point of derision is a sacrilege against the creative spirit, Apollo will eventually punish the blasphemers. The poet then enters into a diatribe against the general abuse of divine forces within the natural world. "Zu lang ist alles Göttliche dienstbar schon / Und alle Himmelskräfte verscherzt, verbraucht" (47:45–47). For "too long," he declares, everything divine has been "serviceable"—the powers of heaven are being ridiculed and abused. Men confuse their superficial scientific knowledge and technological control over nature with a true understanding of it, which can be gained only through religious insight.

In the final three stanzas of the ode, the poet returns to consideration of the behavior proper for poets. It is the ultimate purpose of poetry to evoke and praise the "highest" God, so that this deity may become ever more intimately known by men. God himself will assist them by "covering [their] eyes with holy night so that [they] might remain [living]." Here for the first time in the odes we encounter a theme that becomes increasingly dominant in the later hymns, the dangers of too intense divine presence: just as too much light can destroy eyesight, so too much intensity of divine presence can destroy the lucidity of the soul. Moreover, there is the possibility that someone might (like Empedokles) respond to an overabundance of divine presence with sacrilegious conduct born of overconfidence. The Father does not love what is "wild" or out of control. Thus, the poet continues, it is not good to consider ourselves "too wise." One must instead maintain a stance of proper humility and submissive "gratitude." Yet, while standing before a god veiled in the merciful obscurity of "holy night," the poet may feel terribly isolated from fellow humans; he must thus seek the company of other men whom he might eventually initiate into his own peculiar religious predicament. They might then understand how to help him bear his divinely imposed burden. And still, the poet concludes:

> Furchtlos bleibt aber, so er es muss, der Mann
> Einsam vor Gott, es schützet die Einfalt ihn,
> Und keiner Waffen brauchts und keiner
> Listen, so lange, bis Gottes Fehl hilft. (48:60–65)

(Man however remains, as he must, fearlessly alone before God, innocence protects him, and he needs no weapons and no ruses for the duration until God's absence helps.)

The poet's "innocence"—the quality of total, naive receptivity to divine forces—will protect him from any sacrilegiously cunning or presumptuous attitudes or acts, and he will in fact have no need of "weapons" to defend himself against the deity, or of "ruses" whereby he might attempt to outwit divine power. He must remain in this state of defenseless innocence "until God's absence helps."

This concluding passage is quite mysterious and seems paradoxical; it has given rise to many conflicting interpretations.[12] There is even syntactical ambiguity: one may ask whether "bis Gottes Fehl hilft" means "until God's presence, which we now experience, is replaced by his absence, which will help us," or "until God's absence, which we are already experiencing, eventually helps us." While many critics seem to favor the first reading, it can be argued from the context of Hölderlin's poetry that the second reading is preferable. While in the condition of "holy night," the poet is capable of "knowing" God, not by direct vision or spiritual insight (which has been made impossible) or by conceptualization (which has been deemed illicit), but only through "gratitude"—specifically, gratitude toward a spiritual benefactor who remains otherwise unknown. The poet who stands "alone before God" is thus, in his loneliness, devoid not only of human companionship but of *manifest* divine presence. God may be objectively present, but he is and remains absent to the poet; the holy night is precisely the experience of divine absence. And eventually, it is stated, this absence will "help." Jochen Schmidt refers this statement to the contexts of "Brot und Wein," which elaborates an analogous view of a poet's duties.[13] There (as will be seen in the following chapter) the era of divine absence is viewed as a time of endurance, in which deprivation may eventually so toughen the soul as to make it strong enough again to withstand divine intensity; and, while we are still unable to face the "highest joys" of divine presence, "some gratitude still quietly lives" among us.

The concluding lines of the ode, then, may be regarded as a cryptic allusion to the beliefs more fully articulated in the elegy. The poets must now endure the night of divine absence in innocence and gratitude; eventually the divine absence will "help" us, paradoxically, by making us strong enough to withstand the divine presence, which will be manifest as soon as our capabilities permit. It is, finally, the "poet's vocation," then, to endure deprivation and to proclaim his knowledgeable gratitude toward an obscured God until other men have also come to participate in his attitude so that they, too, may eventually face the presence of the fully manifest "Angel of Day," Apollo, the deity as revealed in light.

The ode "Stimme des Volks" exists in two versions (1800 and 1801), the second being essentially an extension of the first. The poem is a meditation on the destiny of civilizations, which inevitably, according to the will of the gods, must perish as corporate entities. As, however, each civilization may approach its demise either eagerly or hesitantly, the poet speculates on which approach may be more pleasing to the gods. The versions are similar in the first ten stanzas. The first version, however, ends after three additional stanzas of meditative generalizations, whereas the second appends to the first ten stanzas a historical exemplum of eight stanzas, ending in a moral inference.

The first version of the poem begins with an apostrophe to the titular "voice of the people," which, according to an ancient proverb, is the "voice of God."[14] Later in the poem we are given to infer that the divine wisdom allegedly contained in the popular consensus is that of moderation, particularly regarding political change. In the middle of the first stanza, however, the poet abruptly establishes a contrast between "our wisdom" and the attitude symbolized by streams rushing directly toward dissolution in the ocean. Although we may consider their impetuosity unwise, we admire and are moved by them. In their wish to complete their destinies as soon as possible, the streams exemplify a tendency among all mortals to succumb to the desire "all-too-willingly" to fulfill the wish of the gods, taking the shortest path back into the "All."

In the sixth stanza, the poet turns from the metaphor of the stream to generalize on that "deathlust" of nations whereby heroic cities sink into oblivion. He again distinguishes between irrational, unreflective, and uncultivated "nature" and "art" conceived as all that is rational, lucid, and organized. It is the longing for the perfection of nature that leads men to destroy all rational structures and to seek refuge in the oblivion which alone is undifferentiated and therefore perfect. The poet then returns to commemorate those individuals who have accomplished their destinies and gone to rest before their allotted time. They are to be recognized as "first fruits" of the harvest, traditionally offerings to the gods. They will someday be honored as heroic precursors of their respective national destinies. Yet, what is dearest to our mother, the earth on which we live, is for us to be hesitant in our haste, not impetuous like the streams. Such sage moderation is recommended by the common-sensical "voice of the people," and the poet honors its counsels "for love of the gods" in whose wisdom the popular voice shares. Yet, he concludes, the popular opinion tends at times to be too restful, too immoderately moderate, so that people shirk from any action or change. Thus, the poem ends with the wish that "for the sake of gods and men" the people should not "too gladly rest forever."

The first ten stanzas of the second version are virtually unchanged, except for alterations in the fifth and sixth strophes, shortening the allegorical passage on the streams and introducing the theme of national destiny earlier in the poem. These alterations are appropriate here, for (after the tenth stanza's praise of those who fulfilled their destinies early) the poet turns to the historical example of a Greek city. The anecdote is based on fact. According to Plutarch (Hölderlin's probable source), the inhabitants of Xanthos, when besieged and ordered to surrender by the conquering Roman general Brutus in 42 B.C., set fire to their city and chose to die in the flames, though Brutus, concerned for their survival, honestly offered to help them extinguish the fire.[15] The inhabitants of the city thus represent for Hölderlin an extreme instance of men who, by deliberate self-destruction, chose to anticipate in their own destinies the general destiny of Greek civilization. Moreover, the poet is here able to account for the citizens' seemingly senseless behavior. For, he explains, they were merely emulating an episode in their city's earlier history so often retold that it had acquired the status of a heroic legend. In the sixth century B.C., the Persians had besieged Xanthos, and its inhabitants had also set fire to the city and met suicidal deaths. Their descendants were simply acting out the earlier legend.

In themselves, such legends are good because they are a memorial to "the Highest," the transcendent Father-God—they testify to great deeds done in God's honor and at his behest. And yet, the poet warns, there is need of someone to "interpret" these holy legends. If the legend had been properly interpreted, the later Xanthians might have seen that the earlier event should rather be valued as an incentive to moral heroism in general than as an imperative for re-enactment in a merely analogous situation. Whereas the earlier Persian invaders would have destroyed the city and sold its inhabitants into slavery, the Romans were at that time generally willing to leave the local governments and customs of conquered cities intact. The suicidal defiance of the inhabitants in such a situation was thus (at best) ill-considered; they would have benefited from an explication extracting the general moral lesson from the legend while implicitly discrediting it as a model of literal emulation. The second version of this poem, therefore, goes beyond the first in indicating that even the voice of the people, though ultimately coming from God, may sometimes need interpretation by poets.

The final group of odes I will consider were published in 1805. Hölderlin himself in a letter referred to these poems as "Nachtgesänge" ("Songs of the Night").[16] Most of them were probably written in the years of intermittent illness after Hölderlin's first attack of insanity in 1802. While the psychic condition of the poet is not directly relevant to understanding or evaluating these poems, it may help to account for their obscurity and for passages of virtual opacity.

The ode "Chiron," like an earlier version entitled "Der blinde Sänger," deals with the problem of spiritual blindness whereby an individual (such as the fallen Empedokles) is denied the light of divine presence.[17] In the earlier version, the blind singer laments his loss of sight but anticipates the moment when a "redeemer" will come to restore his vision. In "Chiron," the speaker is the legendary centaur who had been accidentally poisoned by one of Hercules' arrows. He, too, deeply regrets his loss of sight as well as the enduring agony caused by the poison. Chiron's eagerly awaited redeemer will also, paradoxically, be Hercules—who, however, will redeem Chiron by releasing him from his immortality, thus permitting him to escape his agony in death.

Other odes published in the "Nachtgesänge" volume include the elegiac "Tränen," which, like so many earlier poems, laments the loss of the gods; "An die Hoffnung," in which the speaker prays for the return of hope; and "Vulkan," addressed to Vulcan as the "friendly fire-spirit" who might comfort us in our present winter of spiritual desolation. "Blödigkeit," like its more exuberantly self-assertive first version "Dichtermut," expresses, however obscurely, a sense of renewed confidence in the poet's vocation.[18] Perhaps the most moving odes in this group, however, are "Ganymed" and its earlier version, "Der gefesselte Strom."[19]

In the latter work, as in "Stimme des Volks" and numerous other poems, Hölderlin utilizes the figure of the river yearning for the sea as a symbol of man's finite consciousness desiring to merge with the absolute. In "Ganymed," although much of the first version's river imagery is retained, the protagonist is identified by the title as the legendary Trojan boy transported by Zeus to Olympus. The stream in the first version, however, is already addressed as "Jüngling." He is first seen as frozen by the cold of winter into icy immobility or sleep. Yet the stream will soon recall its true nature as "son of the Ocean." Even now his father is sending him "messages of love," warm breezes to infuse him with new life. Moreover, the ever wakeful sun-god ("der wachende Gott") is reaching him with his own message of deliverance, his warming rays. Stanzas 3 through 5 describe the melting stream's progressive release from his icy fetters. He awakens from his winter torpor with renewed awareness of his native power and mocks at his shackles, furiously breaking and tossing off the chunks of ice. Soon, playfully exuberant, his demigod's voice awakens the slumbering mountains. The forests and distant cliffs resound to his call, and the joy of springtime heralded by the river's voice stirs again in "the bosom of the earth." The conclusion tells how, by the full coming of the spring, the stream has wandered forth to the immortal ocean:

> Der Frühling kommt; es dämmert das neue Grün;
> Er aber wandelt hin zu Unsterblichen;
> Denn nirgend darf er bleiben, als wo
> Ihn in die Arme der Vater aufnimmt. (2:67)

(Spring comes; new greenery emerges in twilight; but he wanders forth to the immortals. For nowhere may he remain except where the father receives him into his arms.)

Much of the wording of the first version of the poem is ambiguous in that it could refer either (literally) to a personified stream breaking out of its icy confines or (figuratively) to a person overcoming apathy and depression. The person or personified stream is described as exuberantly liberating himself, communicating his exuberance to the natural world, and ultimately finding repose in his father's embrace. The second version, then, is merely altered to enforce the figurative meaning of the poem, converting the personlike stream into a streamlike person.

In the first stanza of the second version, Ganymede is described as *feeling* the cold ("frierst") rather than merely lingering ("säumst") as in the first. Moreover, his mythic identity is brought into play: having (in Hölderlin's adaptation of the myth) returned to a mere earthly existence whose deprivation corresponds to that of winter, he yearningly remembers the time when he had dined on nectar and ambrosia with the gods. Thus in the second stanza Zeus, rather than Ocean, is the "father" who sends him his messages through heavenly breezes. These, as well as a mysterious word spoken to him by a wandering stranger, reawaken divine urgings in his breast, enabling him to overcome the shackles of his despondency just as the stream had thrown off its enshrouding ice. Ganymede's voice, in summoning the natural world back to life, stirs the "spirit in the navel of the earth" to renewed activity. As the "earth's navel" had traditionally been situated at Delphi, this passage may indicate that as Ganymede proclaims his own triumphant anticipation of reunion with the gods, he awakens to new vitality the divine voice of the Delphic oracle, the voice of the god of poetry.

The ode's final stanza is one of the most eerily beautiful passages in Hölderlin's poetry:

> Der Frühling kommt. Und jedes, in seiner Art,
> Blüht. Der ist aber ferne; nicht mehr dabei.
> Irr ging er nun; denn allzugut sind
> Genien; himmlisch Gespräch ist sein nun. (2:68)

(Spring comes. And each thing blossoms according to its kind. But he is far away, no longer with us. He now went astray; for spirits are all too good; now heavenly conversation is his.)

Just as the river finds his destination far away in the embraces of the paternal ocean, so Ganymede is now in the arms of Zeus, eternally departed from this world of cyclical change and rebirth. From a human perspective, he has been taken away, and the gods in their excessive benevolence may have done him a disservice in abducting him to their Olympus. Yet, from his own perspective, Ganymede is now enjoying a sublime communion with gods far preferable to communication with mere human beings. It is not surprising that many readers of this poem have seen in its final stanza an indication of Hölderlin's own acquiescence in what was to be his ultimate (and abiding) fate.

Chapter Six
The Elegies

The *Princeton Encyclopedia of Poetry and Poetics* defines an elegy as "a lyric formal in tone and diction suggested either by the death of an actual person or by the poet's contemplation of the tragic aspects of life. In either case, the emotion, originally expressed as a lament, finds consolation in the contemplation of the tragic aspects of life. In either case, the emotion, originally expressed as a lament, finds consolation in the contemplation of some permanent principle."[1] The ancient Greek elegy was written in a specific verse called the elegiac form; its stanzas were composed of "distichs," pairs of lines, each consisting of a hexameter followed by a pentameter. Hölderlin, following the examples of Goethe and Schiller, adapted this traditional form to his own purposes. He also sought to recapture the spirit of the ancient elegy as expounded by his mentor Schiller in *Über naive und sentimentalische Dichtung,* where the elegy is described as a poem expressing longing for an absent ideal, such as an ideal person or an ideal state or condition.[2] As noted earlier, Hölderlin had experimented with elegiac poetry during his Frankfurt period, but most of these poems could not be considered elegies in the strict sense. He later rewrote one of them, "Der Wanderer," to give it a more distinctly elegiac character.

In its final version, "Der Wanderer" is a poem of six stanzas, each consisting of eighteen lines divisible into three sections of three distichs each, the same organization found in the later elegies "Stuttgart" and "Heimkunft." It is written in emulation of an anonymous Latin elegy, *"Panegyricus Messallae"*: both poems contrast the delights of a geographical temperate zone with the inhospitable extremes of the torrid desert and the frozen arctic region.[3] In Hölderlin's poem, the fictitious speaker—a sailor just returned to his homeland—recalls the unpleasantness of the "African arid plains," where the fire that rains down from heaven is inimical to life. There is, however, too little fire manifest in the arctic zone; consequently, "Mother Earth" has never yet brought forth life there. The speaker celebrates his return home to the Rhineland where, since the sun's divine presence is bestowed in moderation, the green vegetation that symbolizes the pantheistic life of the world is in abundance. He is forced to confront the reality of the fact that his father, his mother, and most of his friends are now dead. But then he realizes that he still has his divine companions: the "Father of the Fatherland," Father Aether himself, as well as maternal Earth and the temperately warm light of the sun. These form a trinity that love and reign over him, and he will never break the bonds of his love for them. It should be noted that the poem's elegiac character does not become manifest until the last two stanzas, where lament for the absent ideal of human love is transformed into joyous consolation through the contemplation of a permanent principle—the abiding presence of the elemental gods.

The first poem that Hölderlin obviously considered an elegy is titled simply "Elegie." It was revised (probably in 1800) and given the title "Menons Klagen um Diotima." In both versions, the speaker laments a lost beloved; in the second, the speaker is arbitrarily assigned the Greek name "Menon," and as in earlier poems, "Diotima" is the beloved woman. The elegy expresses lament not merely for a person but for the kind of ecstatic experience associated with her, for the speaker's love for Diotima is equivalent to his love for the absolute. Although the poem probably had its origin in the time immediately after Hölderlin's forced separation from Susette, its highly idealized mythical context and imagery indicate that it is to be understood not merely as an autobiographical document. It fits the definition of an elegy in that it laments a currently unhappy situation in contrast to an ideal past condition, yet expresses consolation and a hope for a return to a blissful state in the presence not only of the beloved but of the gods themselves.

Several of Hölderlin's elegies were written in Stuttgart in the latter part of 1800. Besides the great elegy "Brot und Wein," they include the fragmentary "Der Gang aufs Land" and the completed but relatively minor poem "Stuttgart." The first of these is addressed to Christian Landauer, a wealthy merchant who was Hölderlin's friend and his host in the city, to commemorate an autumn day when the poet and his friends were to attend a ceremony marking the beginning of construction of an inn on the outskirts of Stuttgart. "Stuttgart" was occasioned by a festive visit to that city by Hölderlin's friend Siegfried Schmid, to whom it is dedicated. The poem does not conform to our definition of an elegy, for there is no element of lamentation. It is a poem of pure celebration, limited only by an awareness that a still greater, more meaningful festivity may lie in the future. It concludes with Hölderlin exhorting his friend to join wholeheartedly in Stuttgart's harvest celebration and to enjoy bread and wine, "the friendly gifts of the god Dionysos." This is not the occasion to speak of what the future holds in store; they will "reserve the greater joy" for their grandchildren.

In some respects, "Stuttgart" anticipates "Brot und Wein." Both deal with festivities presided over by Dionysos, although the Swabian harvest celebration can hardly be compared to the glorious unending feast that constituted Greek civilization. Written probably toward the end of 1800, "Brot und Wein" is usually considered Hölderlin's greatest elegy and one of his finest poems. In it, he most fully articulates his interpretation of ancient Greek civilization and the relationship between that civilization and our own. Greek civilization is viewed as a time of joyous day and of divine presence, which to Hölderlin apparently meant that the gods were literally present and perceptible through the senses. When specific gods are mentioned in Hölderlin's earlier work, they are most often the elemental forces of nature perceived and felt with such spiritual intensity that one is emotionally compelled to recognize their divinity. Aether, the element most frequently apostrophized, is often personified as Father Aether. In "Brot und Wein," Father Aether is celebrated as the principal Greek deity, and the revival of his cult in the modern world is anticipated.[4] In Hölderlin's later work, as we shall see, this originally elemental deity becomes progressively more anthropomorphic and, as "the Father," becomes identified with Zeus and, ultimately, with the Judeo-Christian Father God. It is not wholly clear in "Brot und Wein" whether the other "gods" are elemental, anthropomorphic, or both; perhaps the ambiguity here is intentional.

In any event, Hölderlin here depicts Greek civilization at its height as a world in which men and gods were united in constant festive celebration. In contrast, he depicts the modern world, specifically the Europe of his day, as devoid of all qualities that made ancient Greece a place of beatitude. Whatever gods exist are hidden from us and wholly inaccessible to our feelings, minds, and senses. Because our world is without the light of divine presence, it is a place of deep night, not merely the "darkening plain" of Matthew Arnold's later simile. In this darkness (as in Arnold's), we live in ignorance, confusion, and strife, for there is no illumination enabling us to establish authentic community. "Brot und Wein" is thus primarily about this contrast between the divine presence known to the Greeks and the divine absence experienced by ourselves.

The poem is developed over nine stanzas that can be divided into three

coherent segments of three stanzas each.[5] The first section of the poem
deals with the contemporary night; the initial stanza describes how this
night affects us and how we might respond to it. While many regard night
merely as a time of relaxation, others—such as a "lover" or a "lonely
man"—consider it a time for spiritual authenticity or self-contemplation.
Night is best observed by poets fully aware of its complex symbolical
meaning. In the second stanza, the speaker declares that night's significance is momentous but obscure and thus endlessly fascinating for us; it
gives us not only "forgetfulness" but "holy intoxication"—the "streaming
word" of poetic inspiration and the "holy memory" of departed gods. By
intensifying in ourselves night's gifts of jubilant intoxication, we can
temporarily return in spirit to the time when such ecstasies were known to
all men through their intimacy with the gods. This section concludes with
the poet urging us to return to the holy places of ancient Greece and
hailing Dionysos, god of such holy inebriation, who is prepared to escort
us there.

As the god Dionysos is of central importance for this poem (it was
originally dedicated to "the Winegod"), we might here consider the
significance that Dionysos has for Hölderlin.[6] Unlike that of Nietzsche,
Hölderlin's Dionysos is not opposed to Apollo but is rather Apollo's
nocturnal counterpart. He is not a god of orgiastic violence but rather a
comforting, reassuring deity, a god of lucid poetic inspiration as well as of
alcoholic euphoria. Also, he is here the personification of the spirit of
festive conviviality prevailing among the Greeks and their gods. In his
later poetry, Hölderlin regards Dionysos as a half-brother to Christ and
Hercules, and even in this poem certain passages could refer equally well
to Dionysos and to Christ.

The second section of the poem, stanzas 4 through 6, constitutes
Hölderlin's celebration of Greek civilization. The poet joyously travels
there in spirit, hailing Greece as the house of all the heavenly gods, and
yet, immediately forced to realize that these festivities are long past, he
laments the loss. He then seeks to recall the origin of Greek culture, its
communal recognition and celebration of the Aether as the supreme Father
God, not only as the deity of the sky but as the quintessential principle of
all life. This recognition and celebration constituted the cohesive force of
Greek civilization and brought about the "day" of divine presence and
lucid consensus among them. The central fifth stanza begins by describing
how, when the gods first arrive on earth, they are only vaguely perceived
as a kind of numinous glow. Although, at first, men do not know how to
name them, the spiritual gifts that these presences confer are so gladly

accepted that men begin to "squander" them without proper gratitude. To prevent further misuse of their gifts, the gods then manifest themselves "in truth"—possibly in the anthropomorphic forms depicted in Greek art and literature. The previously unmanifest deities had been named collectively by the concept "One and All," the formula "Hen kai Pan" articulating the pantheistic concept of all-unifying divine life.[7] This transition from a conceptual grasp to an immediate, personal confrontation with the divine is most fully evident in the case of Father Aether. That quintessential element was manifest first as the divinity of the blue sky and ultimately as the anthropomorphic Zeus, the paternal ruler of heaven. When Zeus and his fellow Olympians did appear (Hölderlin continues), they "deeply filled the silenced breasts with free satisfaction and for the first and only time gratified all desire." To greet them, and also to facilitate their manifestation through "naming" them, words had to "originate like flowers" as fully spontaneous expressions of our overwhelming gratitude.

The following strophe recounts the Greeks' joyous response to the epiphany of their deities. In Hölderlin's view, all aspects of Greek civilization—art, literature, religion, political structure, and even modes of behavior—were to be understood as forms of divine worship; it was "in order to stand worthily in the presence of the Heavenly Ones" that the Greek people arose in "splendid orders" and erected their beautiful temples and cities. Yet the poet is again forced to recall that all is irrevocably past; the sacred games are no longer celebrated and the holy theaters are silent. A god no longer might assume human form and, "giving comfort," conclude "the heavenly feast." It might be noted that this passage could refer either to Dionysos or to Christ, since to Hölderlin they are alike in their function as bringers of peace.

The final section of the poem deals with the problems of living in our dark, godless world and seeks a solution in terms of a dialectical relationship between ourselves and the ancient Greeks. Modern poets have no living gods to celebrate; if the old divinities are still alive, they are "above our heads in the other world"—presumably the planets named after them. These deities remain aloof because they know that our eyes, grown unaccustomed to such brightness, would now be blinded by their radiance. Yet the poet is hopeful that at some future time we, like the Greeks, might also have sufficient strength to endure this intensity. We would require a long period of toughening hardship, until there emerge at last "heroes," born in the "brazen cradle" of spiritual deprivation, who are strong enough to be a match for the heavenly ones. Then, the poet proclaims, they would "come in thunder." In the meantime, he asks "why be a poet in a time of dearth?" For it is Hölderlin's conviction that the only fully authentic function of poetry is the praise of *present* deities.

Yet (he continues), poets in our own day may have a somewhat more modest function; they may serve as did the "holy priests of the Wine-god," Dionysos, who in ancient times "wandered from land to land in holy night." In the first section, Dionysos was the god of divine inspiration, giving us the enthusiasm necessary for a spiritual return to ancient Greece; in the second section, he was implicitly the master of revels who presides at the feast of Greek civilization. The third section announces that Dionysos is now to be a cult figure for the present age. Stanza 8 describes the character of the poets' priestly activity. When the gods disappeared from earth and ascended to heaven and "mourning rightly began on the earth," a "quiet spirit" left comforting gifts behind. The spirit is unspecified and, as in the earlier instance, might refer to Christ as well as Dionysos, since both seek to console us for the absence of the gods. The gifts are bread and wine, which, in the Protestant Communion, are consumed in remembrance of Christ; they function as a sign that Christ was once here and will someday return. Bread and wine, however, also had religious significance in the Hellenistic era. The Eleusinian mysteries celebrated Demeter as the goddess of wheat (and therefore of bread), and the Dionysian mysteries celebrated the god of wine. Hölderlin is implying, then, that these gifts have ultimately the same significance within the contexts of both pagan and Christian religiosity. The gifts are not only from Christ but also from the Hellenic gods, and they serve to remind us that *all* the gods were once here and that *all* will someday return. The consummation of bread and wine thus comforts us in our present nocturnal situation, and contemporary poets, as priests of a Christlike Dionysos, have the task of promulgating the message of this consolation and hope.

The concluding stanza of the elegy thus praises Dionysos, who reconciles the day with the night, although we still must wait in our dark underworld until "our Father Aether" is again recognized as a present god. Yet, the poet declares, the "torch bearer," the "son of the Highest," the "Syrian" has already descended among the shades. (This may be Dionysos, who according to some legends was of Oriental origin and who had previously descended to the underworld to rescue his mother, Semele; yet it may also be Christ, for the passage may refer to the legendary "harrow-ing of hell" after the Crucifixion. As elsewhere in the poem, Hölderlin probably intends the identity of their functions as bringers of comfort.)[8]

And, the poet concludes, in this now hopeful underworld, even the infernal dog Cerberus, the spirit of envy and malice, is mollified, drinks of the wine, and falls asleep. The poem thus ends in a mood of quiet consolation and with a new sense of poetic mission: poets are now to encourage our receptivity to hope and to the kind of comfort that ordinary experience, like eating and drinking, can give us.[9]

"Der Archipelagus," though not strictly an elegy, needs to be considered here because of its close thematic associations with "Brot und Wein." It elaborates some of the material presented in the central section of that poem.[10] It has been observed that this lengthy poem is divisible into three unequal sections: lines 1–53, an invocative passage celebrating the god of the sea surrounding Greece; a very long section, lines 54–199, which recounts the history of fifth–century (B.C.) Athens in terms of her relationship with the sea-god; and a concluding section, lines 200–296, presenting the poet's and the sea-god's laments that Greek civilization is no more and (as in "Brot und Wein") anticipating a modern restoration of community in divine presence.[11]

In the first section, the poet declares that in springtime our primal love for nature is rekindled by a resurgence of natural beauty which awakens within us ancestral memories of the age of divine presence. It is always then that the speaker feels impelled to return to the Aegean and to greet that particular sea-god in his now silent divinity. Despite the sea's enduring intimacy with the other forms and forces of divine nature, he feels lonely and unhappy, "for the sacred elements always need for their glory," much as human heroes need human recognition, "the hearts of sentient men." The ancient Greeks provided such recognition for the sea-god and his fellow deities, but modern men are oblivious of the divine qualities in nature.

In the poem's second section, the speaker, as in "Brot und Wein," laments the disappearance of Greek culture and again elaborates on the festive aspects of Greek life (particularly those devoted to the sea-god). He then gives a detailed account of major events in fifth-century Athens. The Persian invasion of 480 B.C. is described as a volcanic eruption destroying everything in its path. The Greeks, however, are that same year avenged at the naval battle of Salamis, where the sea-god himself inspires his beloved people to victory. The poet then describes in considerable detail the return of the fugitive Athenians to their ruined city and their reconstruction of it. Mother Earth provides them with building materials, and to honor her and the "god of the waves" (Poseidon as well as Athena was a patron of the city), they bring a new, more beautiful Athens into being. The new city is the creation of their collective "Genius" that had previously defeated the Persians. The Genius builds it to provide "bonds of love" binding the people to himself.

The concluding section, like the corresponding part of "Brot und Wein," anticipates a new day of divine presence. The poet expresses a wish to seek out the spirits of the ancient Greeks either through death or through a spiritual journey, as in the previous poem. He then, as in "Brot und Wein," returns to the present: Father Aether (Zeus) and the sea-god (Poseidon) are pleading that their divinity may once again be acknowledged. For, the poet declares, "es ruhn die Himmlischen gern am fühlenden Herzen" ("the Heavenly Ones gladly rest on the feeling heart" [2:110]). He again envisions the return of a divinely inspired society under the tutelage of a Father Aether who will unite all men in a universal spirit of communal love. (Here, however, it is stated that the gods themselves might have *need* of *our* love.) Man's present situation is still that of a dark underworld, a nightmarish, roaring "workplace" of aimless, meaningless pursuits. But we will soon be released from this plight: the "beneficent breath of love" will waft among us, and life will again be an unending feast celebrating divine presence.

In the final lines of the poem, the speaker returns once more in spirit to the divine sea. The sea-god himself is immortal, and the poet prays that he might some day hear the resonance of the eternal waves. He wishes that his spirit might dwell on the movement of the sea's surface, its eternal ebb and flow, so that in contemplation he might exert his mind better to understand the ontological nature of temporal process. And if the specific temporality of his own life, his involvement in the often debilitating experiences of history, should prove too shattering for him, he has the recourse of immersing his spirit in the eternal silent depths of the sea.

This poem, like "Brot und Wein," thus has a symmetrical structure. Both beginning and end proclaim the poet's return in spirit to the divine sea of the Greeks. The beginning is followed by a celebration of the festive quality of the Greek world as the end is preceded by an anticipation of an equally festive time that lies ahead. At the center is a historical account of how Athens had prospered through interaction with the gods, perhaps intended as an exemplum of how we too might thrive once divine presence is reestablished. While the two poems are thematically related, their differences are mainly ones of emphasis. Whereas "Brot und Wein" is addressed primarily to the specific problems of poets—the poet's vocation in different eras, the ideal nature of poetic language and its relationship to the divine—"Der Archipelagus" is addressed to the problems and interests of mankind in general. It offers a much more detailed account of how man fares, individually and socially, in a world integrated with the gods and the divine forces of nature.

Hölderlin's last formal elegy, "Heimkunft," celebrates the poet's journey home in the spring of 1801 from Hauptwil. Despite the failure of his third tutorial position, the homecoming was a joyous occasion for Hölderlin, for, the poet reports, he has just experienced a vision of God and is eager to convey it to his beloved kinfolk.

The poem, which retains the verse form of the previous elegies, consists of six strophes, the first of which depicts a symbolic vision of sunrise over an Alpine valley.[12] It begins paradoxically and somewhat obscurely:

> Drin in den Alpen ists noch helle Nacht und die Wolke,
> Freudiges dichtend, sie deckt drinnen das gähnende Tal. (2:96)

(Inside in the Alps it is still bright night and the cloud, composing the joyous, covers the gaping valley within.)

The remainder of the stanza describes the interaction between the clouds and the sunbeams that are beginning to disperse them. The morning is born after a joyous struggle, much as a child is born or as peace emerges from a war. It is obvious that the stanza must be read on a symbolic or allegorical level. As in "Brot und Wein," the Dionysian element is present, for the joyous turbulence is described as "bacchantic." The "bright night" of the valley might share the symbolic value of night in the other poem, just as the depth and darkness of the valley described might suggest the underworld to which our present world has been compared. Moreover, we know that Hölderlin was then delighted by the new peace in Europe; letters of this time indicate an upsurge in his millennial hopes.[13] Thus, the birth of the day from the turbulence of night could be interpreted as the emergence of a joyous era of universal peace in the presence of the gods.

The second stanza reports an actual vision of God, seen as a serenely eternal being residing above all such turbulence. In naming him the "ethereal one," the speaker implicitly identifies him with Father Aether of "Brot und Wein," whose recognition and honor the poet hopes will soon become universal. The deity appears as benevolent; he dispatches lifegiving streams from their Alpine sources and sends forth showers to refresh the land, comforts men in mourning, and occasionally "renews the times" themselves. In the third stanza, the poet recounts the conversation he had

with this deity and his prayer that the advent of the spirit and the return of
the gods might not too suddenly overwhelm the people in his fatherland.
He then turns to his present situation, his crossing of Lake Constance. He
arrives in the Swabian city of Lindau and is ecstatic over the inviting
beauty of the town and the friendliness in people's countenances. Forego-
ing temptations to wander back into the Alps or down the Rhine, the
traveler decides to go directly home, nostalgic for familiar scenes and
expecting to be greeted with great warmth and affection.

The fifth and sixth stanzas anticipate the poet's arrival among his
family, to whom he will relate his encounter with the "great Father who
refreshes wandering Time" and "rules over mountains." He will proclaim
to them that time has now been rejuvenated and that the return of the gods
is imminent. And yet the poet fears that it will then be difficult to find
words to express appropriate gratitude at the new spiritual joy. The
traditional (and, it is implied, no longer adequate) names for God would
now be inappropriate responses from one who has had an intense personal
encounter with the deity, for our joy of gratitude at divine gifts must be
perfectly articulated. Thus, despite the intensity of our joyous feelings, we
must often remain silent in the absence of fresh, authentic divine names.
Whereas the Greeks in "Brot und Wein" were able to name their divinities
in words originating "like flowers," it will be much more difficult for us to
devise words to facilitate a new epiphany of the gods. Thus in the
concluding lines of this poem, the poet must again, as in the previous
elegy, seek some form of consolation. Here the consolations are those of
music: "Aber ein Saitenspiel leiht jeder Stunde die Töne, / Und erfreuet
vielleicht Himmlische, welche sich nahn" (a lyre provides appropriate
strains for each hour and "perhaps" gives pleasure to approaching gods).
Such diversion eases somewhat the "care" about words that has now
disrupted the poet's spiritual joy. Such cares must be the principal concern
of the poet who takes seriously the task of greeting deities about to return
to earth.

This poem thus takes us one step beyond "Brot und Wein." The earlier
elegy had concluded that, while waiting for the gods' return, the poet's
task was to offer hope and comfort to men. In "Heimkunft," however, the
situation is more urgent. The new peace is conducive to the establishment
of harmony and communal love upon earth, a situation that (the poet
hopes) will lead to the appearance of gods in recognition of man's now
perfected spirituality. Yet their epiphany requires an appropriate evocation
by us in wholly appropriate words. Hölderlin's great hymns are devoted
principally to the problems of devising language suitable for such
purposes.

Chapter Seven

The Pindaric Hymns to "Friedensfeier"

It is almost universally agreed that Hölderlin's late hymns constitute his greatest poetic achievement. Those familiar with them are inclined to feel that they may be among the best poetry written in any major European language during the last two centuries. During the nineteenth century, however, most readers judged them wholly incomprehensible and symptomatic of the poet's derangement. Although they are, in fact, extremely difficult, critical studies during the past several decades have succeeded in demonstrating their inner logic and coherence as poetic artifacts. Still, there is no consensus among critics as to interpretation of the more difficult hymns, such as "Friedensfeier," "Patmos," or "Mnemosyne."

Hölderlin's hymns are written in emulation of the fifth-century (B.C.) poet Pindar, perhaps the most difficult of Greek poets, who composed choral hymns (or odes—the nomenclature is ambiguous) to be recited at the celebrations commending athletes who had been victorious at the pan-Hellenic games. His poems achieve poetic greatness through the brilliant complexity of their allusions to historical or mythical personages or events associated with the athlete's city or family. As poems composed for choral recitation on formal occasions, they have been widely imitated in a tradition of Pindaric poetry in post-Renaissance European literature. Unlike most of his modern imitators, Pindar constructed his hymns according to strict formal rules. Each hymn consists of sections (triads) having three stanzas each, with a highly complicated metrical pattern within each triad. Although such a mode of composition is extremely difficult to realize, Hölderlin sought to devise metrical patterns for his hymns that would resemble as closely as possible those employed by Pindar himself.

The question arises why Hölderlin, who by 1800 was the epitome of the subjective, private, even alienated modern poet, would exert himself to write poetry in imitation of one of the most objective, public, and social of ancient poets. The most likely answer appears to be that he then believed that his own function as poet (and the function of modern poetry in general) was about to undergo a fundamental transformation; indeed, a new age of the world was about to commence. As announced in "Brot und Wein," this new age was to be inaugurated by a universal recognition of the divinity of nature and by the reappearance of the gods, who would then need to be greeted at formal public celebrations. There would thus be a need for solemn poetry to be recited in formal articulation of this greeting. We should not conclude that Hölderlin intended that any of his Pindaric hymns actually should be so used. Instead, most of them were written in lively anticipation of the gods' appearance, and the intensity of such anticipation varies from poem to poem. Some hymns probably were intended as public poetry, for they are ostensibly designed to persuade people that the gods' return is imminent and to evoke appropriate enthusiasm. Yet some of the later hymns, though written in the same style, actually express the loneliness of the visionary poet and the anguish of possible uncertainty regarding the interpretation of the vision.

Hölderlin's first attempt at the Pindaric mode, the unfinished "Wie wenn am Feiertage" (1799), is remarkable not only as an experiment in versification; it is one of the most problematic of the hymns and the one in which the divine epiphany appears most imminent. It might even be argued that the present tense, as used in the poem, is a true present and not merely, as in most other such cases, anticipatory.[1] The poem begins with a magnificent epic simile that develops a comparison between "trees" that stand glistening on a brilliant morning after a nocturnal thunderstorm, and "poets":[2]

> Wie wenn am Feiertage, das Feld zu sehn
> Ein Landmann geht, des Morgens, wenn
> Aus heisser Nacht die kühlenden Blitze fielen
> Die ganze Zeit und fern noch tönet der Donner,
> In sein Gestade wieder tritt der Strom,
> Und frisch der Boden grünt
> Und von des Himmels erfreuendem Regen
> Der Weinstock trauft und glänzend
> In stiller Sonne stehn die Bäume des Haines:

> So stehn sie unter günstiger Witterung,
> Sie die kein Meister allein, die wunderbar
> Allgegenwärtig erzieht in leichtem Umfangen
> Die mächtige, die göttlichschöne Natur. (2:118)

(As when on a holiday, to see the field, a countryman goes in the morning, when from hot night the cooling lightning bolts fell the entire time and the thunder still sounds from afar, the stream steps back into its banks, and the ground greens freshly, and from the joy-giving rain of heaven the grapevine drips, and gleaming in the quiet sun stand the trees of the grove:

Thus do they stand under favorable weather, they, whom no master alone, whom the mighty, the divinely beautiful Nature educates, wondrously all-present, in gentle embraces.)

Both are presented as standing under favorable weather conditions; the now radiant trees have stood intact during a severe storm whose rain has refreshed all of nature, while the poets (we learn later in the poem) have experienced analogous conditions in their lives. "Nature" is here, as in *Hyperion* and *Empedokles,* the "all present," and "divinely beautiful" pantheistic life of the universe; she has spiritually "educated" all true poets in her loving embrace. Because of the intuitive rapport between Nature and her poets (the second stanza continues) the poets feel withdrawn and alone during periods—such as the winter of the year or the spiritual winter of our present age—when the divinity of nature is not manifest. Yet both the poets and Nature herself during such times will always "anticipate" the reawakening.

This awakening is announced in the poem's remarkably ecstatic third stanza.

> Jetzt aber tagts! Ich harrt' und sah es kommen,
> Und was ich sah, das Heilige sei mein Wort.
> Denn sie, sie selbst, die älter denn die Zeiten
> Und über die Götter des Abends und Orients ist,
> Die Natur ist jetzt mit Waffenklang erwacht,
> Und hoch vom Aether bis zum Abgrund nieder
> Nach vestem Gesetze, wie einst, aus heiligem Chaos gezeugt,
> Fühlt neu die Begeisterung sich,
> Die Allerschaffende, wieder. (2:118)

(But now it dawns! I waited and saw it coming, and what I saw, may the Holy be my word. For she, she herself, who is older than the times and is above the gods of the evening and orient, Nature is now awakened with the clash of weapons, and from high in the Aether to down in the abyss, according to fixed law, as once before, engendered from holy Chaos, inspiration, the all-creating one, feels renewed.)

The manifestation of nature's divinity has now dawned upon the world, and the poet prays that his "word" may be sufficiently "holy" to proclaim her adequately. She is hailed as older than all the ages of this world and, as divine life itself, superior to all particular manifestations of that life, the individual "gods." She now has been awakened by the "sound of weapons," the wars (believed by Hölderlin and many of his contemporaries to be apocalyptic) unleashed by the French Revolution. These wars are analogous to the violent thunderstorms in the natural world, and the "inspiration" occasioned by them and the consequent awakening of nature is implicitly described as a thunderbolt produced by the "holy chaos" of a storm. Such inspiration is the present manifestation of the "all-creating" demiurge that, operating according to fixed laws, originally constituted the ordered structures of the phenomenal world. Thus, it is implied, the inspiration that poets presently feel is comparable in its divine intensity to this primal force. The speaker then proceeds to elaborate on the poets' current illumination: their souls have been set aflame with enthusiasm occasioned by the apocalyptic "deeds of the world." Now attuned to nature's divinity, they are able to perceive the divine character of elemental forces previously regarded merely as objects of technological exploitation.

In the fifth stanza, the poet instructs the reader where these divine forces are to be manifest. Their "spirit" is to be present in "song" engendered by the "sun of the day," by the "warm earth," and by "storms"—not only atmospheric phenomena but also analogous disturbances in the human realm, the "thoughts of the communal mind," articulations of the *Zeitgeist*.[3] Such thoughts, in comparison to the physical storms, are "more prepared in the depths of time" and "more meaningful and more perceptible to us." They "wander forth between heaven and earth and among the nations" as ideological principles conducive to violence. Yet such ideas must terminate with quiet yet powerful impact in the "souls of the poets," like lightning-bolts igniting the "fire" mentioned above. Under ideal conditions, a poet's soul would then tremble at a sudden "remembrance" of previous acquaintance with divinity and, "enflamed by the holy bolt" of the Father (God), would, like a pregnant woman, give birth to ideal "song." Such song would be a "fruit born in love," the offspring of divine inspiration and the poet's own soul. We are then offered a figurative mythical analogue for such a miraculous birth:

> So fiel, wie Dichter sagen, da sie sichtbar
> Den Gott zu sehen begehrte, sein Blitz auf Semeles Haus
> Und die Göttlichgetroffne gebar,
> Die Frucht des Gewitters, den heiligen Bacchus. (2:119)

(So fell, as poets say, when she desired to see the god visibly, his lightning on Semele's house, and the divinely struck bore the fruit of the thunderstorm, the holy Bacchus.)

According to one account, Dionysos was the child of Zeus (the storm-god) by Semele. Semele foolishly desired to behold her divine lover in his full glory; the god reluctantly agreed, and Semele was destroyed by the fiery intensity of divine presence, although her child was rescued from the flames. It is thus that ideal poetry could be produced by the impact of the divine lightning-bolt on the poet's soul—significantly, this stanza makes no reference to the fate of Semele herself.

As in "Brot und Wein," Dionysos is not only the god of wine but the deity dwelling in wine itself; here he is also compared to the joy conveyed by ideal poetry. But the most significant comparison in this poem is that between Semele's conception and bearing of Dionysos and the ideal poet's inception and production of ideal poetry. Thus, the seventh strophe suggests that just as Semele was the agent through which ordinary mortals, "the sons of earth," now drink the "heavenly fire" contained in wine without danger, so should the poets now be agents producing poetry that would make elemental divine powers manifest to other men. Therefore, the speaker exhorts, the poets are to stand fully exposed to "God's thunderstorms," the violent intellectual disturbances of the time, that they might be receptive to "the Father's bolt," the divine "thought," or activating principle of these disturbances. The poets must fearlessly seize this thought with their own hands and encase it in their "song" to be conveyed to the people so that the divine spirit might be communally shared. And, ideally, the poets should have nothing to fear. If they are but innocent and as pure-hearted as children, and if their hands are unsullied by guilty action, the equally "pure" bolt will not harm them; moreover, their hearts will remain "firm" ("fest"), even though deeply shaken by a traumatic participation in the mighty agonies of a far stronger god.

Then, however, the tone of the poem changes abruptly. The speaker exclaims "weh mir" ("woe is me"), and a lacuna appears in the manuscript. The lacuna corresponds to the following passage in an earlier prose draft of the poem:

Aber wenn von selbstgeschlagener Wunde das Herz mir blutet, und tiefverloren
der Frieden ist, u. freibescheidenes Genügen, Und die Unruh, und der Mangel
mich treibt zum Überflusse des Göttertisches . . . (2:669–70)

(But when my heart is bleeding from a self-inflicted wound and peace is deeply
lost, and freely-allotted contentment [is lost], and unrest and want drive me to
the superabundance of the god's table . . .)

It will be recalled that, although the poet has compared the role of the poet
vis-a-vis the father god to that of the mythical Semele, no reference has
been made to her fate in the myth. The seventh stanza had delineated
ideal conditions for the poet's encounter with the god, conditions that
would assure the poet's safety. The speaker now seems compelled to
consider the alternative. If the poet's hands, which should be innocent,
are instead guilty of an unholy act that has resulted in the poet's loss of
peace and contentment—then he might be motivated to seek solace by
forcing himself upon the gods and their graciousness rather than (as one
should) merely inviting the gods to approach at their will. However real
and intense the suffering of such a man, the gods would resent and
punish the hubris of his intrusion. Following the manuscript gap, the
later version of the poem goes on to describe the punishment he would
then deserve as a "false" priest unworthily seeking his own gratification.
The gods would cast him deep into the darkness of despair, just as they
had punished acts of hubris by the legendary Tantalus or Sisyphus. Then
he would sing a "warning song" urging other would-be hierophants to
avoid his fate. At this point the poem breaks off, obviously unfinished.

As mentioned earlier, this poem is not only difficult but highly problematic. It might be asked why the poem breaks off where it does and why
there is an abrupt shift in the unfinished eighth stanza from the "we" of
poets in general to the "I" of the particular poetic speaker when the poet
turns to consider the alternatives of the "false priest." This shift has led
some critics to conclude that Hölderlin is here speaking of himself and of
his own exposure to hubris after the "self-inflicted wound" of his parting
with Susette Gontard.[4] Hölderlin might thus have been unable to
continue the poem because his own involvement in the mythos made
further objectivity impossible. However, it should be pointed out that
the passage considering the false priest is in the conditional subjunctive,
indicating mere possibility rather than actuality. Moreover, it could be
argued that dialectical tensions within the poem itself prevented its
continuation after this point.[5]

Another incomplete hymn, written perhaps a year later than "Wie wenn am Feiertage," is the much more fragmentary "Der Mutter Erde," which, according to the poem's fictive structure, was conceived as being alternately recited by three fictitious brothers, Ottmar, Hom, and Tellos. It is much too incomplete to merit consideration in detail; of significance, however, is Tellos's declaration that the Father God has decreed that Mother Earth should now be accorded the highest honor and should be the recipient of songs "in his name." The paternal deity remains ever more "hidden" and absent to us, whereas Earth is eternally present in her holiness. Thus, she must take his place for a while as the recipient of the highest worship until the soul of man attains its full spiritual potential and the other gods are sent to us again.

The unfinished hymn, "Am Quell der Donau" (written probably in 1801) addresses, like "Brot und Wein," and "Der Archipelagus," our relationship to ancient Greece. Here, however, our relationship to ancient Asia is also considered. As the poem's two opening stanzas were never cast into verse, their content must be inferred from a prose draft.[6] In the draft, the poet first hails "Mother Asia" as a presence thousands of years old and full of "heavenly fire," the intensity of divine presence. The voice of ancient Asia still reaches us and still anticipates an authentic response, a "resonance of love" from a living breast. An appropriate metaphor for such a response might be the Danube River, which has its source ("Quell") in the poet's Swabian homeland and, unlike most German rivers, travels in an easterly direction toward the Black Sea.

Following this initial lacuna, the extant poem consists of seven stanzas. The first of these utilizes an extended simile like that of the "Feiertag" hymn. The divine voice of Asia is here compared to the powerful music of a church organ playing a prelude on the morning of a feast day, awakening a house and its inhabitants and filling them with "inspirations." The chorus of the community, thus brought together by the force of music, can then articulate a proper response to the rising sun. Like such inspiring music (the poet continues) "came the word from the East to us." This holy word was our "awakener," the "voice that forms human beings" ("Die menschenbildende Stimme"). As in *Hyperion,* it is here implied that men become fully human only through active participation in divine presence. Much of Hölderlin's philosophy of history is implicit in the account presented here of the course followed by this voice before it reaches western Europe.[7] Full awareness of divine presence is seen as having had its origins in Asia (perhaps among the Hebrews) and is conveyed by Asia's voice in a westerly direction. It comes first to the

Greeks, the first Europeans to develop a full human culture, then to Rome and her empire, and eventually to "us" over the Alps—perhaps in the Renaissance, when northern Europe for the first time began to realize the worth of the ancient civilizations.

However, northern Europe's first response to the discovery of classical culture was one of benighted confusion. The poet declares that we did not then achieve clear understanding of the divine spirit informing Greek culture nor did we in the intervening centuries. We have exhausted ourselves in the mastery of the world and are too fatigued by pragmatic exploits to appreciate the deities that have been revealed. In this poem, the full epiphany of the divine to us is seen as occurring at the evening of the day, corresponding to the end of a historical era, whereas in "Brot und Wein," our situation had been presented as a night wherein we await the dawn of the gods' return. Here, they will return (presumably) at sunset, a moment of illumination corresponding to the golden age at our era's dawn. This historical metaphor will also be used in the important hymns "Der Rhein" and "Friedensfeier," where its implications are explored in more detail.

After praising the joy of the ancient Greeks and the noble spiritual endurance of the Hebrew prophets, the poet then calls upon all the ancients collectively:

> . . . Aber wenn ihr
> Und dies ist zu sagen,
> Ihr Alten all, nicht sagtet, woher?
> Wir nennen dich, heiliggenötiget, nennen,
> Natur! dich wir, und neu, wie dem Bad entsteigt
> Dir alles Göttlichgeborne. (2:128)

(But if ye—and this is to be said, all ye ancients—did not say whence we name thee: [then] under holy necessity we will name thee, Nature, and freshly, as from a bath, there will arise for thee all that is of divine birth.)

This extremely difficult passage contains two different forms of the vocative, differentiated in my translation by *ye* and *thee*. The ancients ("ye") are urged by the poet to tell him the exact source ("whence") of the name ("Nature") for the divine all-unifying life of the world. But if the ancients cannot or will not reveal their source, then contemporary poets ("we") will be compelled by divine inspiration to pronounce a new name for the life designated by "Nature," and the new name will have power to

provide this divine life with a fresh revelation of all the particular forms—
that is, all the individual deities of the various nations and cultures—in
which this life had been manifest. The poet's highly ambitious concern
with the ultimate naming of "Nature" was already prominent in the
"Feiertag" hymn (where its articulation was hoped to engender the
ultimate "song") and was to dominate some of the hymns that follow.

In the sixth stanza, the poet offers another simile for our present
situation. Although spiritual "orphans," we have inherited from the
Greeks the "weapon of the word," the holy instrument of ancient poetry
which may provide us with a means of coping with divine powers. Yet, the
poet confesses, we are less adept ("Unge*schick*ter") at using such verbal
weaponry than the ancient "children of destiny" ("*Schick*salsöhne")
who—as the German pun suggests—were *destined* to be *skilled* in the
divine art of poetry.[8] Thus, in the concluding stanza, the poet, abandoning his attempt to compose an objective hymn, makes a subjective
admission of failure. He confesses that the very intensity of his involvement with divine forces has now so overwhelmed him that he cannot
continue the poem, for the hymn has turned into a highly personal love
song toward the divine spirits. Moreover, he laments, "everything goes
that way"—his present involvement with the gods being such that he
finds it impossible ever to escape from subjectivity.

"Die Wanderung," probably composed in the same year, is perhaps
Hölderlin's first completed Pindaric hymn. Although it makes no major
poetic statement and is considerably lighter in tone than the other hymns,
it is thematically related to the previous poem. The first two stanzas are in
praise of Hölderlin's native Swabia, hailed as "blissful" and the poet's
"mother." Despite the beauties of his native region, the speaker here, as in
many other poems, desires to travel eastward, for he has recently heard a
theory about the origin of the ancient Greeks. According to that theory,
the Greeks were descended from a union between Germanic people ("das
deutsche Geschlecht") and another unspecified race ("Kinder der
Sonn"). The poet presents a whimsical account of the initial encounter
between them and then plaintively asks where these "dear relatives" now
live, so "that we might again celebrate the alliance and remember the
dear ancestors?"[9] As if seeking reunion with these "relatives," the poet
once again recalls the festive life of ancient Greece, here equated with an
eternal song of joy. This time, however, he would like only to pay a short
visit there, merely to summon their "Graces," the "*Charitinnen*" (spirits
who preside over festivities of gods and men),[10] and invite them to
return with him to Swabia "if the journey is not too far." The poem

concludes with a meditation on the paradoxical qualities of such divine visitation: heavenly moods such as those conferred by them are very elusive and not to be attained by force or trickery. Like Christian "grace," they are always bestowed gratuitously.

We might now compare the poetic statements made in the two hymns just discussed. As already observed, both belong to the large group of poems delineating the poet's attitude toward ancient Greece. "Am Quell der Donau," however, does not, like "Die Wanderung," express desire for a spiritual journey; rather, it prescribes how we should respond to our sacred legacy from the ancient world by devising a new poetic name for "Nature." In this emphasis it differs from "Brot und Wein," where the primary poetic task (other than giving human comfort) was the reestablishment of the recognized divinity of Father Aether. This change of emphasis was already signaled in "Der Mutter Erde" with its declaration that primary honor should be given to the maternal Earth—like "Nature" a feminine concept of the divine, immanent rather than transcendent.

In the hymn "Germanien," also probably written in 1801, the poet is again concerned with the proper relationship between ancient Greece and modern Germany. Here, however, as in the ode "Gesang des Deutschen," Hölderlin expresses the belief that Germany may some day enjoy the level of intimacy with the gods, and of general culture, equal to that known by ancient Greece. In the first stanza, the poet (after describing his country's spiritual condition as analogous to that of a sullen afternoon threatened by storms that could bring either destruction or welcome rain) laments that his desire to conjure up the spirits of the Greek gods has become a temptation almost too powerful to resist, despite the baleful consequences of any yielding to it. For, it will be recalled, the unholy desire to behold overpowering divinities was the temptation to which the "false priest" succumbed. And, as in "Brot und Wein," the poet still feels not "strong" enough to encounter the gods. It is, of course, still permitted to *think* of the ancient deities, and in the second stanza, the poet hails the anthropomorphic gods of the Greeks as "fled" from the world (no longer specifically "dead" as in the first stanza). He also greets deities who are still "present" but were in olden days "more truly real" ("wahrhaftiger")—presumably the elemental natural forces worshiped by Empedokles. After reflecting on the demise of Greek religious cults, the poet declares that the gods may be about to visit the earth anew. These "Göttermenschen" may be interpreted here either as anthropomorphic deities (such as Apollo, Aphrodite, etc.) or as virtually divine human beings, such as are envisioned in *Hyperion*. Such gods, whom it would be fatal to conjure up, would sanctify us at the moment of their arrival. In the third stanza, then, the speaker tells how Germany is prepared to receive such divine guests. The landscape is ready to welcome them, and on "prophetic mountains" one may stand gazing eastward in anticipation of their arrival.

Then, from the middle of the third stanza to the end of the poem, the poet presents the allegorical tableau of an annunciation. Two characters are involved: an eagle—traditionally an emissary of Zeus—and the maiden "Germania," personifying Germany. Here, the eagle conveys the will of the Father God as "Lord of Time," director of historical process. The eagle (like the "menschenbildende Stimme" in "Am Quell der Donau") has visited, in turn, those countries or regions where divine revelation was most intense and most productive of high culture: first ancient India, then Greece, and then the Italy of the Roman Empire.[11] Immediately after the fall of Rome, Germany was not yet ready for his message, and the eagle did not then fly over the Alpine peaks.[12] Now, however, the time is right, for he triumphantly crosses them to behold the German provinces awaiting his arrival.

The fourth stanza introduces the Germania who will allegorically represent the poet's fatherland in receiving the eagle's message. Jochen Schmidt argues that the Latin name, as well as many details in this poem, indicate that the poet is here thinking of Tacitus's *De Germania,* written toward the end of the first century A.D., in praise of the noble simplicity, integrity, and primitive virtues of the Germanic peoples.[13] Hölderlin, drastically revising the view of the Germans presented at the end of *Hyperion,* now attributes these qualities to his present compatriots as collectively personified by Germania. She is thus described as "the quietest daughter of God," who "too gladly keeps silent in deep simplicity." The eagle, upon finding her, delivers the speech that constitutes the remainder of the poem.

The speech is an annunciation analogous to that delivered to the Virgin Mary by the angel Gabriel. The eagle begins by hailing her as chosen because of her "all-loving" nature. She has now become strong enough to endure a "heavy good fortune"—that is, she is now safely receptive to divine presence. Because of her profound spiritual kinship with all-loving Mother Earth, she is to devise a new name for this deity, thus fulfilling the desire expressed in "Der Mutter Erde"—Earth's hidden essence is now to be made manifest. Yet, the poet cautions, this name is too sacred to be enunciated; it must remain "unpronounced" even though Germania, as in ritual magic, must "thrice describe it"—thus naming Earth indirectly. Such naming (like the naming of nature in

"Am Quell der Donau") will result in a renewed manifestation of all forms of the divine, for Earth will effectively give birth again to the old gods, and the coming future forms of the divine will also appear and speak to us. Germania herself will then become the source of all wisdom for mankind and preside over the festive harmony that is to reign among them:

> Bei deinen Feiertagen
> Germania, wo du Priesterin bist
> Und wehrlos Rat gibst rings
> Den Königen und den Völkern. (2:152)

(At your holidays, Germania, where you are priestess, and, defenseless, give counsel round about to the kings and the nations.)

Hölderlin's hymn "Der Rhein" (also probably written in 1801) is generally deemed to be one of the poet's greatest achievements.[14] It consists of fifteen stanzas, clearly divisible into five sections of three stanzas each. Hölderlin has left us a cryptic and somewhat obscure note delineating the structure of the poem.[15] The first two sections of the poem (stanzas 1–6) present a symbolic interpretation of the course of the Rhine River in terms of a type of human "destiny." This interpretation raises the issue of hubris, which had been a dominant theme in the Empedokles drama. The third section of the poem (stanzas 7–9) deals with this topic in a general manner. In contrast, the fourth section (stanzas 10–12) considers the specific case of the philosopher Rousseau, who avoided hubris despite divine gifts that could have led to his downfall. The final section (stanzas 13–15) describes a "bridal feast" (prophesied and to some extent prepared by the writings of Rousseau) that will be the ultimate reconciliation between men and gods.

The first section begins with the poetic speaker recounting a past experience in an Alpine setting:

> Im dunkeln Efeu sass ich, an der Pforte
> Des Waldes, eben, da der goldene Mittag,
> Den Quell besuchend, herunterkam
> Von Treppen des Alpengebirgs. (2:142)

(I sat amidst dark ivy at the portal of the forest, just as the golden midday, visiting the source, came down from the steps of the Alpine range.)

At noon, the sunlight, descending along the peaks, is preparing to enter the deep glen where the source of the Rhine is hidden. The poet himself is sheltered from the light and surrounded by ivy, emblematic of Dionysos and the poetic priesthood of offering comfort while yearning for the gods' return. The Alps are for him "the divinely built . . . fortress of the Heavenly ones, according to old opinion, where much that is decisive succeeds in secret to men." As in "Heimkunft," they are the refuge of the gods on earth and the optimal sites of divine visitations. The poet is now about to witness such a visit; for, as he sits pensively, almost yearning in spirit for ancient Italy and Greece, he suddenly and "unsuspectingly perceives a destiny." This destiny is the birth and the subsequent course of the Rhine, the child of Father Aether ("der Mittag") and Mother Earth. He thus typifies the ideal demigod; for Hölderlin—here and in later poems—a demigod is any offspring of a heavenly (divine) father and an earthly (mortal) mother. The Rhine's destiny is thus, in this poem, presented as typical of the destinies of demigods in general.

The second stanza consists of a single sentence depicting the heroic agonies of the newborn Rhine, who in his deep gorge is raging at his dark confinement away from the paternal sunlight, the divine origin that he painfully remembers in his present misery. For demigods, while aware of their dual nature and parentage, may be violently unhappy in early life. The following stanzas explain and comment on the Rhine's thwarted desires. He is, in fact, the "noblest of the streams," born with a clear sense of the godlike freedom of his will. Unlike his brothers, the Ticino and the Rhône (also born in the Alps), the uncompliant and "impatient" Rhine is driven eastward toward Asia by the impetus of his "royal soul." Impelled through awareness of his origin, he seeks the place of primeval divine immediacy. The Rhine's destiny is thus intuitively perceived by the poet just at the moment when he felt an analogous yearning for Greece. Yet, "wishing," the poet then declares, "is unwise in the face of destiny," for one's will is inevitably thwarted. A demigod's will to freedom and self-realization is so intense, however, as to make him impervious to actuality. Thus the young Rhine vehemently wills an easterly course until "experience" of encounters with barriers compels him to flow in a north-westerly direction.

In the fourth stanza (opening the second section of the poem), the poet continues his reflections on the Rhine's intransigence. "What is of pure origin (*Reinentsprungenes*)," he asserts, "is a riddle." The true nature of the river's divine origin can hardly be expressed even in the most inspired language. But the effects of such an origin prevail throughout life:

> . . . Denn
> Wie du anfingst, wirst du bleiben,
> So viel auch wirket die Not,
> Und die Zucht, das meiste nämlich
> Vermag die Geburt,
> Und der Lichstrahl, der
> Dem Neugebornen begegnet. (2:143)

(For as you begin, you will remain; and, even [regardless of] how much effect
necessity and discipline exert, [one's] birth has the greatest effect, and the beam
of light that encounters the newborn one.)

It is the initial impetus of the soul—one's birth and the beam of light (in
this case, divine) that first strikes the newly born—that determines the
character of an individual's life, rather than the distress and discipline that
may keep that impetus from self-realization. The Rhine would seem
especially determined "to remain free his entire life" and to fulfill nothing
but his "heart's desire." For he had the best conceivable origins—his
divine father descended from a propitious height and he himself was born
most fortunately from the "holy womb" of his Mother Earth. "Therefore"
(the fifth stanza continues) "his word is a jubilation." Full of joyous
enthusiasm, he has the prowess of a young Hercules.

In his first exploit, the infant Hercules had exuberantly slain two
enormous snakes sent to kill him in his cradle. Likewise, the Rhine also is
not merely content to "cry in swaddling-bands like other children." When
the river's steep banks threaten to close in upon him like constricting
serpents, his response is the same as that of Hercules: "laughingly he tears
up the snakes" and dashes away. After this heroic victory he feels he cannot
be checked on his course toward Asia. Yet he must be curbed; otherwise, if
permitted to grow in speed and momentum to the force of a lightning-
bolt, he would, in a violent Oedipal union, "split the Earth," and woods
and mountains would follow him as if enchanted into the abyss. Thus, in
order to prevent this catastrophe and to spare his son, the Rhine's divine
father intervenes by setting up the massive obstacle of the highest Alps to
block his course. (Hölderlin is here perhaps referring to the bend of the
Rhine near Chur, Switzerland, where the river veers decisively northward.)[16] The god then "smiles" at his son's raging frustration and his
wrath against his father's will, for such frustration is a purification
process through which the Rhine is compelled to chastise his own will
and harmonize it with reality. Thus, tempered like a sword by the
ordeal, the Rhine flows quietly northward and finally, as a great river,

northwest through Germany itself. In his final, mature phase, the Rhine sublimates his divine longings through useful activities, providing a source of water to the surrounding countryside and serving as an avenue of commerce for his "children," the cities along his banks.

The third section of the poem, dealing with the problem of the demigod's temptation to hubris, begins in the seventh stanza with a comment on the Rhine's later contentedness: "Doch nimmer, nimmer vergisst ers." A demigod like the Rhine should never forget his divine origin and the "pure voice" of his intense youthful desires for divine immediacy; it would be better for him even to destroy all ordering structures of human life. (The poet is here not advocating the nihilistic alternative but merely emphasizing that forgetfulness would be even worse.) The rest of the stanza indicates conditions under which temptations to such violence may arise. It may happen that the "bands of love" (the cohesive forces within a civilization originally founded through communal spirit) become "fetters" restricting freedom and self-realization. In such cases, demigods like the older Rhine may feel the excessive intensity of their youth revive and, moved to defiance through their deep love of freedom, may challenge a civilization's basic laws. Since these laws are divinely ordained, they will thus invite the "heavenly fire" of the gods' revenge.

In the next stanza, the poet examines the *proper* relationship between men and gods and explains how this delicate relationship is disrupted. The gods, he declares, have "enough with their own immortality, and if they are in need of anything it is heroes, men, and other mortals." For the gods, though immortal, are unreflective and have no self-consciousness or "feeling."

> . . . Denn weil
> Die Seligsten nichts fühlen von selbst,
> Muss wohl, wenn solches zu sagen
> Erlaubt ist, in der Götter Namen
> Teilnehmend fühlen ein Andrer,
> Den brauchen sie. (2:145)

(For because the most blessed ones feel nothing of themselves, another must [if it is permitted to say such a thing] participatively feel in the gods' names. Him they need.)

Although the poet is reluctant to attribute any deficiency to the gods, he thus suggests that they may need to make use of the self-consciousness of mortals who can sense the presence of the gods *within* themselves and, by "feeling in the gods' names," bring the deities within them to self-awareness. However, the men whom the gods have chosen for this purpose are subject to the temptation actually to believe themselves to be these gods—the error that consummated Empedokles' hubris in the play's first version. Then, in the assertion of their assumed divinity, such men become impassioned "ravers" and regard all "bands of love" as fetters blocking their self-aggrandizement. Their punishment is that they themselves destroy their own homes and see their friends and families perish; this is the "judgment" passed by the gods upon a *Schwärmer* who "wants to be like them and not tolerate inequality" with the gods.

In stanzas 7 and 8, the poet thus explores the possible destinies of demigods whose sense of divinity gets out of control, yet he declares that even their lot would be preferable to that of one who forgets his origin entirely. In the ninth stanza, he contemplates the golden mean achieved by the Rhine, who has discovered a "well-allotted destiny" and can think back nostalgically on his past wanderings and hardships. Such a man has attained a "secure shore" and can behold about him the territory God preordained for him at birth. Then, like the elder Rhine, he can rest, blissfully contented, for the divine presence he once so urgently sought in its unmediated form now surrounds him mediated (and diffused) through the serene happiness of his mature life.

In the hymn's fourth section, the destiny of Rousseau is presented in terms analogous to that of the Rhine. The poet confesses his difficulty in coming to terms with Rousseau's fate. While demigods such as the Rhine move him deeply to sympathize with their fates, Rousseau is such a strange figure that the poet scarcely knows what to call him. Hölderlin here speaks of Rousseau much as he had previously spoken of Empedokles: through intimacy with the gods Rousseau's soul had been strengthened by the ordeal of divine presence until it became unconquerable. He was, moreover, gifted with a "sure mind" and "sweet gifts" both to hear the gods and to convey their messages to other men. His prophetic utterances, however, sometimes had unfortunate effects. In this respect, Rousseau resembles the Empedokles denounced by Hermokrates for betraying divine mysteries to the masses. However, the poet expressly absolves Rousseau of any personal guilt for calamitous results springing from his teachings. Rousseau spoke in all innocence from a Dionysian fullness of inspiration. His words were fully intelligible to men of good will but benighted those who misinterpreted and thus desecrated his teachings—for example, the more extreme "Rousseauistic" ideologues of the French

Revolution. Because of his uncanny gifts and his power of influencing men's minds, Rousseau thus seems an enigmatic "stranger." (However, we may note, this strangeness may also be due, paradoxically, to the uncanny kinship of spirit Hölderlin felt toward Rousseau. It should be recalled that in the ode "Rousseau" he ascribes to him the role of prophet of approaching gods, which in "An die Deutschen" he had reserved for himself.)[17]

The eleventh stanza continues the poet's meditation on the Genevan philosopher. Like the ideal poets foreseen in "Brot und Wein," Rousseau's soul had developed sufficient strength to endure divine presence. Yet such strong poets may assume the burden of comprehending divine life to a greater extent than even they are capable of withstanding. As demigods, aware of their divine origin, they are also aware of their sonship to Earth. Thus, as "sons of the earth," they emulate their mother in taking on the full burden of "Heaven," the paternal divine presence, for they are "all-loving" toward transcendent life. When, however, such a demigod becomes aware of the weight of "the Heaven, which he has with loving arms heaped upon his shoulders," and of the correspondent intensity of his own response, the "burden of joy," he may be surprised, even terrified, by a greater magnitude of divine presence than he can emotionally or conceptually endure. It may then "seem best" for him temporarily to rest from his high responsibilities. Thus Rousseau, after numerous persecutions because of his disruptive teachings, found temporary respite and peace on an island in Lake Bienne, Switzerland, where (as he relates in his autobiographical writings) he spent his days idling amidst the beauties of nature. Yet, Hölderlin implies, Rousseau's period of rest does not involve even a temporary abandonment of the poetic vocation. Rather, in a situation of reverie, a condition much like that of the poet himself in the first stanza, and shielded from the intensity of divine presence, Rousseau spent his time learning to compose in a naive mode wholly attuned to the simple harmonies of nature.[18]

The poet then recounts how Rousseau, arising from the "holy sleep" of his reverie, emerges shortly before sunset from the coolness of the forest to encounter the "milder light" of the evening sun. This is no ordinary sunset but, like the sunset in "Am Quell der Donau," signifies the glorious end of our present era. As earlier in the poem, the sun or "the day" ("der Tag") is the image of the Father God, who is here again descending to maternal Earth, but in a gentler fashion. Having created the world and guided its destiny throughout the centuries, he is now going to rest. He is returning to Earth not as to his spouse but as to his "pupil" whom he had shaped or formed, and he now finds "more good than evil" in the world he made.

The poem's concluding section is devoted to the "bridal feast" to be celebrated in the golden hours of this sunset. The gods will be reconciled and reunited with men at the end of our era, just as they had been in its beginning. All living things—gods, men, and nature—will "celebrate," and destiny will be "settled for a while." Destinies (such as the Rhine's) had been the result of separations between men (or demigods) and their divine source. These destinies will be resolved now that the father has returned. Men will be affected in various ways at the festivities, but all will be reconciled as the spirit of divine inspiration, like an evening breeze, murmurs about the dark trees. Even enemies will "hasten to extend their hands to each other" before the friendly light goes down and the night comes. For this new golden age of divine presence is here perceived as being as transient as it is glorious.

Moreover, the fourteenth stanza indicates, the "friendly light" of divine presence at sunset will be experienced longer by some than by others; although universal, it is a subjective event, and its duration cannot be measured by objective time. Such divine life, eternally enjoyed by the gods, is necessarily fleeting for men. Yet a man who has once experienced this "best" of moments can keep it alive in his memory until death, "and then he will experience the highest." The poet here repeats the observation made earlier in "Brot und Wein": everyone has a limit or "measure" ("Mass") of how much divine life he can endure at any time, whether at the "midday" of intensity or the "midnight" of deprivation. There are, however, some individuals exceptional in their stamina:

> Ein Weiser aber vermocht es
> Vom Mittag bis in die Mitternacht,
> Und bis der Morgen erglänzte,
> Beim Gastmahl helle zu bleiben. (2:148)

(But a wise man was capable of remaining lucid at the banquet from midday into midnight and until the morning gleamed.)

The poet is here referring to Socrates, who in the banquet described in *The Symposium* remained clearheaded and discoursed on topics such as divine beauty long after other guests had passed out from excessive drinking. He thus typifies the ideal instance of someone who has great capacity ("Mass") for divine life and is able to maintain the "Best" in memory at all times, even when other men have lost that capability. He is (possibly) presented to us as a model for emulation during the times both preceding and following the bridal feast.

In the hymn's concluding stanza, another model is presented, Hölder-lin's friend Isaac von Sinclair, to whom the entire hymn is dedicated.[19] Sinclair is visualized first in an Alpine setting similar to that of the first stanza, in warm shade, then in the cooler seclusion of a German oak forest. In either situation God may appear to him in the steel armor of a medieval knight (as Sinclair was both a visionary and a militant revolutionary, it is fitting that the deity should appear to him as a god of heroes). Or God might appear to him more conventionally in "clouds." Either vision would be possible for Sinclair, for he knows God as the "power of the Good." He thus at all times enjoys the favoring light of divine presence—the smile of the God who directs history is upon him both day and night. Day is here the time "when the living appears feverish and enchained," held captive beneath the world's phenomena, whereas night is the time "when everything is mixed without order and age-old confusion returns." This description, which (like the entire stanza) is extremly difficult to interpret, may refer to the night that will follow the bridal feast. It is likely that Hölderlin was thinking of a figurative chaos in which men (totally deprived of light) would experience a total confusion of beliefs and values with no recourse to transcendent ideas. In such a benighted age, Sinclair, like Socrates, would retain his moral lucidity, for even then he would be able to perceive his God smiling upon him. Like the Rhine, he would come through all his ordeals safely and perhaps (as suggested through the analogy with Socrates) he or his spirit might survive to behold a new dawn of divine presence.

We noted earlier that "Der Rhein," like "Am Quell der Donau," effects a revision of Hölderlin's metaphor for the historical process, making our present situation analogous to the time just before sunset. However, this poem develops more thoroughly than the previous hymn the implica-tions of this symbolic revision. The substitution of sunset for sunrise on one level poses no problems: both are beautiful moments when earth and sky are filled with golden light, and both are times of pleasantly moderate coolness. Both are also moments in which the sun (the divine) and the earth (the realm of mortals) appear to be on the same level. For all these reasons, both moments are appropriate for indicating a time of joyous rapprochement between men and gods. However, the implica-tions are greatly different in the two cases. The dawn symbolism (im-plicit also in the "Feiertag" hymn and "Heimkunft") was less problema-tic: our present night will be followed (it seems to be implied) not merely by a dawn but by an entire day of divine presence.

These poems thus display relatively uncomplicated historical op-timism. "Der Rhein," however, and several other late poems, pose serious problems of interpretation. Daytime obviously cannot signify a simple lack of divine presence, for the sun is a traditional symbol of deity, which appears to be utterly consistent throughout Hölderlin's work. However, Hölderlin (whose psychic condition was gradually worsening) was increasingly coming to regard overly intense, unmediated divine presence as a threat. Thus in this poem, the speaker, Rousseau, and Sinclair are all significantly ensconced in protective shade. The situation in "Germanien" was that of a late afternoon with heavy clouds both covering the sun and heralding a storm. And in "Friedensfeier," as we shall see, the festivities are to occur at sunset immediately *after* a thunderstorm. In these hymns, the human condition is thus regarded as a time threatened either by harsh sunbeams or by lightning-bolts; Hölderlin uses the word "Strahl" indiscriminately to indicate both. Also, the transiency of the sunset celebration gives a somewhat gloomy undertone to the conclusion of "Der Rhein," as do the questions the reader must pose regarding the nature and duration of the coming "night"—which, as an unambiguous emblem of divine absence, could hardly be an unequivocal improvement upon our present day. All these problems must be taken into account by interpreters of "Der Rhein" and some of the poems that follow.

The hymn "Friedensfeier" was probably written in 1802 to commemorate the Peace of Lunéville, which ended one phase of the Napoleonic wars. However, the manuscript of the finished poem was not discovered until 1954 (earlier fragmentary versions of the poem had been published previously). The poem, perhaps the most difficult of Hölderlin's hymns, thus first became known at a time when many scholars had already arrived at definite positions concerning his work. It was thus inevitable that it should become the object of controversy and that, with its many disputed passages, it should be interpreted in a wide variety of ways.[20] The following discussion, then, should be read merely as an abbreviated version of one possible interpretation. It might be noted that Hölderlin, in a preface to the poem, virtually concedes its strangeness and difficulty.[21]

The poem, like many of the hymns, is composed of triads, with twelve stanzas divisible into four sections. Like the concluding section of "Der Rhein," it is dedicated to an anticipated celebration that will unite men and gods in festive harmony. However, it greatly exceeds the previous poem in the scope of its description and interpretation of these festivities. The first three stanzas describe the setting of and preparations for the feast and speak (in nebulous terms) of its appointed "prince," or master of ceremonies. Critics have disagreed whether the first stanza, which describes the feast's intended setting, depicts a room, a landscape after a storm, or both. It seems safest to interpret the passage as describing the landscape in terms of a hall. It is to this festive landscape that "loving guests," the gods, have come "at the hour of evening."

The second and third stanzas are devoted to the poet's distant perception of the "prince" of the celebration. As the prince is here described in ambiguous terms, critics have vehemently disagreed as to his identity. Interpreters have identified him variously as Jesus Christ, Napoleon Bonaparte, the sun-god Helios, the Spirit of Peace, Dionysos, and even the Spirit of the German People.[22] And it must be said that for most of these identifications persuasive arguments can be made on the basis of textual evidence both within and outside the poem. The second stanza is obscure and has been diversely interpreted. Some information can, however, be derived from it. The prince is a stranger among us who has just accomplished a heroic feat; he now takes on the form of a kindly youth, even assuming an attitude of demure modesty. Yet the poet recognizes him as one so famous as to be known by all. The prince is no mortal, but a god who instantly inspires adulation and provides illumination that no human could offer.

The third stanza continues the description of the prince. He is not "of today" nor is he "unheralded." In his heroic exploits, he had avoided neither "flood nor flame." He causes astonishment now that it has become "quiet," and with good cause, "since dominion is nowhere to be seen among spirits and men." His militant heroism has somehow resulted in a total peace in which all authority and inequality have been abolished. For, the speaker explains, men can now for the first time hear the "work" ("das Werk") that has been long in preparation "from morning until evening." This work can be perceived because the thunderstorm (already suggested in the first stanza) is now past—no ordinary weather disturbance, but a "thousand-year storm" which had been "the Thunderer's echo." The storm passes off to sleep, "reverberating in the abyss" with its distant rumblings now drowned out by sounds of peace. The stanza closes with the poet's appeal to all his friends to join with him in the imminent festivities.

It is clear that Hölderlin is once more speaking in terms of historical allegory. The thunderstorm, which in the "Feiertag" hymn symbolized the revolutionary wars, here signifies the entire span of Western civilization. This had been a violent era in which the prince, it is suggested, had taken a leading role. The "flood and flame" he had endured can be understood as the torrents and lightning-bolts of the millennial storm. The peace celebration over which he is to preside will perhaps also (as in

Christian tradition) be millennial, certainly not merely (as the Peace of
Lunéville proved to be) a brief pause in hostilities. The character of the
"work" accomplished and now completed is still mysterious, but it is
clear that it will be marked by peace, harmony, and equality. It later
becomes clear that the "work" is the product of the storm itself and that
it designates the harmonious totality of earthly existence during the
coming era.

Stanzas 4 to 9 form a conceptual unit enunciating the gist of the
poem's prophetic message. It is in this section that the meaning of the
feast and its prince is (however obscurely) expounded. As this exposition,
however, is not linear, the section can be interpreted only by examining
the complicated thematic references in the various stanzas. Thus, the
fourth stanza begins with the poet speculating upon the question of who
should be invited to the feast and who should be the guest of honor. It
becomes clear that the most honored guest should be Christ. The poet
here refers to Christ's encounter with the Samaritan woman at the well,
an incident in which Christ's "friendly-serious" attitude toward men is
exemplified. Christ is described as "shaded" both by the nearby sacred
mountain of the Samaritans and by his own disciples, who constituted a
"loyal cloud" that obscured the "holy-daring beam" of his divine
radiance. It is here implied that the full significance of Christ's life and
teaching has been historically diminished and distorted through the
mediation of his disciples. And yet, the poet laments, Christ was more
drastically overshadowed by his own death, which occurred before his
entire message could be enunciated and was thus "fearfully decisive" for
the later development of a Christianity based on an incomplete and
impaired understanding of Christ's teachings. Thus, the poet concludes,
"everything heavenly is quickly transient"—and yet "not in vain."

For, as the poet declares in the fifth stanza, the gods are always cautious
and "sparing" in their visitations so that their intensity may not be deadly
to man. Thus, the misinterpretations to which Christ's nature and teachings were subjected were actually ordained by providence out of consideration for man's spiritual incapacity. Proper gratitude at Christ's benefice to
us has been impossible as long as the gift itself has remained misunderstood; its true significance can be grasped only after deep and prolonged
reflection. Yet, we are again reminded, if Christ had not been historically
"sparing" in his benevolence we would long ago have been destroyed, just
as a benign hearth fire can destroy a house if it gets out of control.

Yet, the sixth stanza continues, "Des Göttlichen aber empfingen wir /
Doch viel": we still received a great deal of divine benevolence visibly

mediated to us in the elemental presences of nature. All elements, however, are but aspects of the "all-living" Father God (whose divine life informs all things), the giver of our joys and of our inspired songs. He has, throughout history, begotten a number of "sons" or demigods, one of whom (Christ) is characterized as "quietly powerful." And, the poet continues, we now, for the first time in history, can "recognize" ("erkennen") Christ's true nature and significance since we "know" ("kennen") the Father as the principle of all-unitive life rather than as the authority figure of Christian orthodoxy. Moreover, that aspect of the Father which controls the historical process, the "Spirit of the World," has now descended among us "to celebrate festive days" ("Feiertage zu halten"). This divine Spirit, then, who has come to earth to instigate festive celebrations, appears to be the "Prince of the Feast" already partly described in the poem.

In the seventh stanza, the poet describes the interaction between this Spirit and the world:

> Denn längst war der zum Herrn der Zeit zu gross
> Und weit aus reichte sein Feld, wann hats ihn aber
>   erschöpfet?
> Einmal mag aber ein Gott auch Tagewerk erwählen,
> Gleich Sterblichen und teilen alles Schicksal. (3:535)

(For he was long too great to be Lord of Time and his field extended afar; but when did it ever exhaust him? But for once even a god might choose a day's work like mortals, and share all destiny.)

Utilizing a complex spatial metaphor for temporal duration, he declares that the Spirit had long been too great to correspond exactly to the "field" of historical process. Now, however, history, reaching its conclusion, is approaching its ultimate goal. The "field" then is viewed as a historical day's work for the Spirit. As the third stanza's prince, he had been the controlling intelligence of the millennial day's thunderstorm. Since the storm is now over, the Spirit is prepared to descend to earth and "share all destiny."[23] The law of this destiny had ordained that throughout the storm all men must gradually come to know one another, so that, when the serene "silence" of peace would return to the world, there would "also be a language." From the following stanza, we learn that this ultimate language would be that of "song," while the previous era's language had been that of "conversation." As the present stanza observes, the discussion had been highly polemical: "Wo aber wirkt der Geist, sind wir auch mit, und streiten / Was wohl das Beste sei" (But wherever the Spirit is working, we are also along and dispute what the Best might be). The focal point of mankind's continuous debate during the millennia of divine occlusion has been the question of the nature of the highest good. The Spirit has been managing this dispute and the wars of truth that it has often enkindled. Now, however, the argument is settled, for the highest good is now manifestly revealed to us all. The poet thus now considers the present moment to be the epiphany of the much-disputed "Best." This epiphany is here depicted as a completed "image" or picture that the master painter, the Spirit, has prepared in the workplace of world history. As the next stanza indicates, the Image is the "Time-Image," the entirety of history viewed esthetically as a finished artifact. Having put the finishing touches on this picture, then, the Spirit emerges from the process now radiantly "transfigured" by his own work as a quiet god of time. His emergence as a tranquil deity is appropriate, for the "law of destiny" of the stormy era is now superseded by the "law of love," a beautifully reconciling influence now in effect both on earth and in heaven—a spirit of universal benevolence under whose aegis (as the third strophe observed) all authority and inequality can be abolished.

The eighth stanza elaborates on the implications of the seventh:

> Viel hat von Morgen an
> Seit ein Gespräch wir sind und hören voneinander,
> Erfahren der Mensch; bald sind wir aber Gesang. (3:536)

(Much, from morning on, since we have been a conversation and hear from one another, has man learned; but soon we are song.)

Mankind as a whole has come to full self-knowledge through *being* the conversation whereby individuals could hear from one another from the very morning of our era. "But soon," the poet declares, "we will be song." Our linguistic mode of existence will be transformed from one of discourse to one of unending melodious praise to the gods—such is the "language" that the previous stanza had predicted would emerge at the return of tranquillity. And, the poet continues, the "Time-Image which the great Spirit discloses" will not only be a comprehensive depiction of the historical process and its triumphant result but will also function as a "sign that, between him and others, is an alliance between him and other powers."[24]

The Image shows that there is an alliance between the Spirit of history and the elemental divine presences of nature; for the natural elements with which man has always worked have played integral and essential parts in man's history. Thus not the Spirit alone but "all the unbegotten, eternal ones are recognizable therein," just as the elements of earth, light, and air have contributed to, and are recognizable in, the lives of plants. Yet, the poet declares, his most favored metaphor for the consummation of history remains not the time image but the "feast day," the "sign of love" for the gods and the testimony that they are still present and beloved by men.

The feast day (the ninth stanza continues) will be the "all-gathering" occasion for all the previously occluded gods. Because their attendance must be complete and because, above all, "their most beloved one, on whom they depend" must not be missing, the poet now must issue the invitation tentatively extended in the fourth stanza: Christ himself must now be summoned to the festivities. The poet magniloquently calls upon Christ to come to the prince of the feast.[25] Now that we fully know the Father God and understand the workings of his Spirit in the historical process, we can fully and safely recognize for the first time the entire meaning of Christ's life and words. We can understand fully his proclamation of the "Law of Love" at the Last Supper, as we have finally, through the guidance of the Spirit, established the complete rule of this law upon earth. We now wholly understand, and fully honor in songs of lucid gratitude, the Father, the Son, and the Holy Spirit. And not only these traditional aspects of the Christian God but *all* the gods ever recognized, honored, and worshiped by man are now to be present to us on our own dwelling place, our earth.

The problematic final section of the poem recedes somewhat from the triumphant tonality of the ninth stanza. In the tenth, the poet returns to his own actual temporal perspective, the time of anticipation preceding the feast. This stanza achieves an effective evocation of the mood of joyous expectation and tells how all men wonder at the radiant freshness after the storm and how each secretly anticipates the great joy that is to come. This expectation is of such strength as to restrain the oldest men from dying.[26] The next stanza then observes that "troubles prepared from above and also carried out" are the "spice of life." The many sufferings and anxieties of the previous era make us now appreciate even more our simplest joys, for we are confidently awaiting the vision of the gods, whose epiphany has been "long sought-for."

In the concluding stanza, the poet reflects upon our initial loss of the ancient gods.[27] "Nature," divine life as mother of all beings, cried lamentation like a "lioness" when she lost the gods, her children, from the world. For, being all too loving, nature had treated her "enemy" almost as if he were one of her own children; she had thus in effect induced the gods to associate with "satyrs." Nature's enemy is here to be understood as the violently egotistical negative tendency within man himself.[28] This spirit, active in man, had once deprived the world of gods through its unbelieving arrogance. Yet, the poet continues, nature has repeatedly given birth to and buried many beings. Many of these deaths can be attributed to the same cause, for nature, though all-powerful and eternal, is yet hated by that negative principle she herself once raised into the light. But nature herself now recognizes, and is resigned to, the inevitability of cyclical death and rebirth, and, the poet obscurely concludes, "that which is anxiously busy below gladly rests without feeling until it is ripe." The gods' new epiphany is, at this moment, still in the seminal phase and will remain dormant until it emerges to full glory. From this conclusion it thus appears that the poet's initial mood of elated certainty about the imminence of the gods' return has, in the course of the poem, yielded to an awareness that there may yet remain a time of waiting before their arrival. The poet's implicit anxiety, muted here, will become more evident in the hymns that follow "Friedensfeier."

Chapter Eight
Later Pindaric Hymns and Other Poetry

Although "Friedensfeier" was the most triumphantly affirmative of Hölderlin's Pindaric hymns, the poet ultimately became dissatisfied with its conclusions. In the fragmentary hymn "Der Einzige," the first version of which was probably written in 1802 after Hölderlin's first attack of madness, he drastically put into question the previous poem's assurance that mankind would soon be treated to a vision of Christ reconciled with all the other gods. Indeed, he here laments his inability to envisage Christ amidst the Greek pantheon.

As reconstructed by Beissner, "Der Einzige" consists of three fragmentary versions that are virtually identical in their first four stanzas.[1] In the first version, as in the others, the speaker begins by posing a question:

> Was ist es, das
> An die alten seligen Küsten
> Mich fesselt, dass ich mehr noch
> Sie liebe, als mein Vaterland? (2:153)

(What is it that chains me to the old, blessed coasts, so that I love them even more than my fatherland?)

Ten years earlier, at the time of writing the Tübingen hymns, this question would have been merely rhetorical; now, however, it has a deep, personal meaning for the poet. In earlier poems, Hölderlin had proclaimed that his own fatherland was about to become the site of a divine epiphany that would rival that of ancient Greece; in "Germanien" he had expressly forbidden himself to look backward toward the gods. Now, however, the strength of his continuing emotional attachment to Greece has become so strong as to be overwhelming and involuntary. He feels as if he were "sold into heavenly captivity." Despite such coercion, the speaker is now fully present in spirit in that world for which he had so often yearned. And yet, he laments, invoking the gods and heroes, one particular manifestation of the divine could not be known among the ancient Greeks:

> Noch Einen such ich, den
> Ich liebe unter euch,
> Wo ihr den letzten eures Geschlechts
> Des Hauses Kleinod mir
> Dem fremden Gaste verberget. (2:154)

(I yet seek one whom I love among you, where you hide the last of your race, the jewel of the house from me, the foreign guest.)

As the next stanza indicates, this last and most perfect embodiment of divine presence, apparently not to be found among the Greek deities, is Christ.

The poet then invokes Christ in the traditional terms of *Master, Lord,* and *Teacher* and confesses that, although he has long endeavored to discover Christ's presence in the world of Greek antiquity, he has failed to devise a way of interpreting Christ in the context of that world. Moreover, the poet admits, his failure in reconciling Christ to the other gods is his "own fault"; his enduring emotional attachment to Christ has been too strong. And yet, in keeping with his notion of the common paternity of all demigods, he still must boldly assert that Christ is "brother" both to Hercules and to Dionysos, even though he remains emotionally incapable of fully accepting this truth. He then must confront the problem of this conflict between his feelings and his ideas, which has turned this poem into a mere confessional lyric.

In the remainder of the poem, the poet speculates on the nature of his attachment to Christ. Both Christ and the other demigods ("Helden"), he declares, experience earthly existence as a kind of capitivity. Like the youthful Rhine, they are, in the midst of their activity, yearning for reunion with their Father in heaven. Thus, despite his accomplishments in effecting his Father's will, Christ too was troubled by the confines of worldly existence. In concluding, the speaker extends this kinship of earthly dissatisfaction to include poets like himself: "Die Dichter müssen auch / Die geistigen weltlich sein." This difficult sentence may be translated as "the poets, the spiritual ones, must also be worldly," and may be interpreted to mean that poets, like Christ and the other demigods, are condemned to live in this world, thereby experiencing the frustrations and limitations of earthly life, which may thwart their "spiritual" endeavors.[2] The experience of "heavenly captivity" described in the hymn's opening stanza is thus transformed into an experience of "worldly captivity" in the conclusion. This sharing in the frustrations of existence is at the root of the poet's intense sympathy with Christ, and it is thus, in the poet's estimation, the ultimate cause of this poem's failure as a hymn.

The hymn "Patmos," unlike "Der Einzige," is so successful as a hymn that many readers consider it Hölderlin's greatest poem.[3] It may owe its origin to a request by Hölderlin's benefactor, the pious Landgraf of Homburg, for a poem to strengthen his Christian faith in the face of a world ravaged by a decline in traditional values.[4] This poem, probably composed late in 1802 and presented to the Landgraf on his birthday in January of the following year, most likely puzzled its recipient with its abstruseness. Yet, however obscurely, the poem is indeed concerned with Christ and speaks of his life, death, and inevitable return in glory. The apocalypse predicted in the final section is somewhat more in keeping with Christian tradition than that depicted in "Friedensfeier," for Christ is here indisputably at the center of the event; yet, this hymn (like most of Hölderlin's later poetry) is decidedly heterodox in its doctrinal implications.

In the poem's initial stanza, the speaker finds himself alone and confronted with a dilemma perhaps even more painful than that expressed in "Der Einzige." This dilemma is enunciated in the highly problematic opening lines:

> Nah ist
> Und schwer zu fassen der Gott.
> Wo aber Gefahr ist, wächst
> Das Rettende auch. (2:165)

(Near is the God and difficult to grasp. But where danger is, grows also that which saves.)

The difficulty of the passage is partly resolved if we understand the "God" not as any particular manifestation of divinity but as Hölderlin's supreme deity, the all-unifying life of the cosmos. While the *dangers* of the intense presence of this life have often been acknowledged in Hölderlin's poetry, his poetry has also shown concern with the *difficulty* of attaining any cognitive, emotional, or intuitive "grasp" of this deity.[5] The Greeks had been able to comprehend this god under the name "Father Aether," but this name, like the name "God" itself, has (as "Heimkunft" implies) lost its evocative power for us. There is thus the danger not only that we might be destroyed by unmediated life but also that we might despair of finding modes of language that might (as anticipated in the "Feiertag" hymn) safely mediate this life for ourselves and others. Such language, the ultimate "Gesang" of "Friedensfeier," is thus presumably "das Rettende" which (the poet assures us) is gradually coming into being in the very midst of our doubly precarious situation.

The following lines of the stanza describe a stark Alpine landscape with high peaks separated by deep gorges, emblematic of extreme fragmentation. Yet eagles (emissaries of Zeus) dwell in the dark crags and are able to cross between peaks in flight, as do the peasants on rope bridges, heedless of the danger of falling into an abyss. The scene's meaning is then explained. The mountain tops are the "peaks of time," and upon each peak is someone "perishing," actually at a short distance from the others though "most separated" by the gorges. Although the designation is highly problematic, these "peaks of time" may perhaps be understood as those moments, whether in world history or in the life of an individual, when we are closest to the all-unitive "God," and when we most intensely experience deity as near and difficult to grasp. At such moments, each individual may perish in his isolation, for, as indicated in "Brot und Wein," an all-unifying deity can be apprehended only by a community; an individual cannot endure the divine presence alone. The opening lines of a later version of this stanza read, "Voll Güt ist. Keiner aber fasset / Allein Gott" (2: 179) ("Full of goodness is [God]. But no one can grasp God alone"). Those isolated on the various peaks are "most dear" to one another because of their mutual "nearness" and their common endeavor to grasp the deity. They are thus potentially capable of communal apprehension of God, if only their mutual isolation could be overcome. The poet concludes the stanza with a prayer for water (presumably to fill up the gorges) or for "wings" such as eagles possess so that those heretofore isolated might establish a communion, each "going over" but also "returning" to his peak in awareness that the task of comprehending the deity is not only common to all but proper to each individual at his own historical moment.

As the following stanzas indicate, at least part of this wish is immediately (and unexpectedly) granted to the speaker. An eaglelike spirit ("ein Genius") seizes him and carries him off through time and space from his own "house" (i.e., his proper time and place) to the ancient world of

Asia Minor, where he had "never thought to come." He arrives there at the moment of sunrise and, at first "blinded" by the unaccustomed radiance of intense light, immediately begins to seek something that he knows, for he is bedazzled and confused by the glare of the sun and by the beauty of the landscape. The radiance of divine presence here is immediately sensed as too dangerously intense for him. Thus, in the fourth stanza, he seeks to escape westward across the Aegean. This direction ultimately would lead him homeward; yet he first seeks refuge on the island of Patmos. Paradoxically it is Patmos's extreme poverty and desolation, atypical of the Greek islands, that most appeal to him, for he finds these qualities congenial to his own spiritually desolate and impoverished state. He thus chooses as the most accessible peak of time the Greek island that is most associated with Christianity; for Patmos had once offered her bleak hospitality to another fugitive, the aged apostle John, who was still in mourning for his "homeland" and for his "departed friend," Christ. The poet, in distant commiseration, thus focuses his attention on John and, through much of the remainder of the poem, virtually adopts as his own John's point of view: John's remembrance of Christ, his experience of Christ's departure and its aftermath, and his apocalyptic expectations, which ultimately are merged with those of the poet himself.

It was traditionally believed that John was the disciple who in his youth had been closest to Christ. John most cherished his memory of the Last Supper, when Christ most completely revealed himself to his disciples and most clearly enunciated the nature of divinity:

> . . . und es sahe der achtsame Mann
> Das Angesicht des Gottes genau,
> Da, beim Geheimnisse des Weinstocks, sie
> Zusammensassen, zu der Stunde des Gastmahls,
> Und in der grossen Seele, ruhigahnend den Tod
> Aussprach der Herr und die letzte Liebe, denn nie genug
> Hatt' er von Güte zu sagen
> Der Worte, damals, und zu erheitern, da
> Ers sahe, das Zürnen der Welt.
> Denn alles ist gut. (2: 167)

(And the attentive man beheld accurately the face of God when, at the mysteries of the grapevine, they sat together at the hour of the banquet, and in his great soul, quietly anticipating, the Lord pronounced death and the ultimate love, for he then never had enough of words to say about goodness and to cheer, when he saw it, the raging of the world. For All is Good.)

He there foretold his own death and enunciated the "ultimate love," giving the commandment that his disciples should love one another as he has loved them; for "greater love hath no man than this, that a man lay down his life for his friends" (John 15:12–13).[6] Throughout this Gospel chapter, Christ, as reported by John, reiterates the supreme "goodness" of God's (and of his own) love for men in the face of the "world's" rage. For, the poet declares, "All is Good." Although this statement is not actually attributed to Christ in the Gospel, it represents for Hölderlin both the underlying assumption and the essential summation of Christ's teaching: that despite the world's rage, all things are ultimately pervaded by God's goodness and love. Such an assurance not only is compatible with traditional Christian belief but also is implied in Hölderlin's own pantheistic understanding of God as all-unifying life.[7] Hölderlin thus implies that Christ, confronting his own imminent death at the Last Supper, achieved the ultimate articulation of the concept of God as all-unity in his formulation of the law of supernal love.

The poet then tells of the disciples' last glimpse of Christ as he gazed upon them in the "joyous" triumph of his final victory over death and the world. And "yet," (the seventh stanza continues) the disciples "mourned now that it had become evening," for the focal point of their lives had suddenly been taken from them, ending their (and mankind's) day of divine presence. They were thus not yet ready to acknowledge their "greatly decisive" destiny—to lay the foundations of Christianity, even though most of them would thereby suffer martyrdom. They were also understandably reluctant to leave their native land, so closely associated with their many remembrances of Christ. It was to disrupt their passivity and inertia that Christ "sent them the Spirit" at Pentecost. This event is here interpreted as Christ's final appearance to his apostles, imparting his own Spirit to them. Just as Empedokles had to die before his spirit could be released to his followers, so also with Christ, and for the same reason: the religious leader, as object of passive adulation, had to disappear before his informing spiritual principle could be actively and subjectively experienced by each of his followers. At Pentecost, then, the disciples, forcibly inspired, became "heroes" indifferent to death in their zeal to spread Christ's word. They were caught up in the "storms of God," collectively the "thousand-year storm" which, according to "Friedensfeier," was to be guided by the "Spirit" throughout the Christian era.

And yet, the eighth stanza relates, the presence of such subjective inspiration within the disciples was offset by the utter loss of divine presence in the phenomenal world. Moreover, the Spirit compelled their dispersal throughout the world so that Christ's words might be preached to all men, thereby forcing them to depart from one another and from their beloved homeland. The tenth stanza, then, poses a series of questions regarding not only this necessary evil but also the entire problem of the meaning of the world's spiritual history since the time of Christ. The disciples, who had "lived together in memory," gradually became "enigmas" to one another, as each evolved his own private (and distorted) understanding of Christ and his teachings. Thus were inaugurated the confusions and the mutually contradictory interpretations of Christ that were to characterize the entire "Christian" era. Not even a proper memory of the divine could be preserved in this period, in which the force of history seems a raging desert wind sweeping before it all that is holy, so that "nothing immortal is anymore to be seen in heaven or on the green earth." What, then, the poet asks, is the ultimate meaning of this apparently horrible world destiny?

The eleventh stanza proposes an answer in terms of an elaborate metaphor. The process of history is like the toss of a shovelful of wheat across a threshing floor, during which the heavier chaff falls to the ground, while the wheat ("das Korn") scatters to the ends of the floor. The shovelful of wheat mixed with chaff signifies Christ's teachings as misinterpreted from the time of the apostles, whereas the chaff signifies the errors and irrelevancies that have crept into Christian doctrine. This chaff will eventually be discarded, allowing the grain (the full, uncorrupted truth of Christ and his teachings) to emerge purified at the end of the process. Presumably, this truth will be the full realization of the ultimate insight enunciated by Christ at the Last Supper, the idea that all is good, the cosmos pervaded by all-unifying divine life. Even if some of Christ's teachings must remain obscure to us, we should not be dismayed: "For divine work also resembles our own; the Highest does not want everything at once." It will be enough if the essence of Christ's truth is made clear; God, like men, may be content with some momentary imperfections.

The poet next considers a possible temptation to construct for himself an "image" of Christ to comfort him while he awaits the culmination of history. He would have sufficient wealth of spiritual insight to fashion a picture that would look much as Christ appeared while alive. However, in an obscure passage (even the syntax of the lines is conjectural), the poet warns that possessing an image of Christ (or of any deity) might induce us to attempt to become godlike through servile imitation of this image. Any such attempt would, of course, be blasphemous and would infuriate the gods themselves. For what they hate most is any human counterfeiting of the divine. Moreover, such hubris would make us ignore the necessity of being merely human servants of the gods' will. For, the poet continues, not men but "the immortals' destiny" is in control of the historical process, now rapidly approaching its triumphant conclusion, at which time the victorious Christ will be appropriately "named," allowing his divine glory to be as manifest as the sun. This naming (the thirteenth stanza continues) will be as a "password" admitting mankind to the millennial feast. In anticipation of this naming, the poet now receives from the gods "the staff" of the universal "song" foretold in "Friedensfeier," which will serve to beckon the gods to descend to the feast. For, the speaker declares, "nothing is common"—no aspect of life is now to be seen as trivial or meaningless; all things are imbued with divinity.

Yet, man's present situation is still like that of the underworld described in "Brot und Wein." The staff of song will first have to awaken many still "dead" to any divine presence. Moreover, many who await the light of the returning gods with "reticent eyes" may (like the poet himself) seek comfort in the gently mediated light of divine truth revealed in "Holy Scripture." In the fourteenth stanza, the speaker turns to address his patron, the Landgraf, himself a devout student of Scripture. The gods, he declares, love the Landgraf for his devotion to the Father's will, manifest not only the Bible but in a "sign," the lightning-bolt, which paradoxically "stands silently" amidst the "thundering heaven" threatening our present situation. This divine sign has been manifest throughout the stormy Christian era. And "one man," Christ, has been standing beneath it his entire life, for "Christ is still living" in our world. Here it is thus Christ himself, rather than the "Spirit" as in "Friedensfeier," who is the moving force of history. His continuing function as direct recipient of supernal divine power is similar to that role to which the poet aspired in "Wie wenn am Feiertage." Yet, even here, the poet observes that Christ is not the only person to convey his Father's will. The events of history, particularly those instigated by demigods as conscious agents of God's will, have provided commentary both on the meaning of Scripture and on the lightning-bolt as the most intense form of private inspiration. But the Father himself is immediately involved in historical process, for through divine foreknowledge, "his works are all known to him from perpetuity."

In the poem's final stanza, the speaker once again turns to our current situation of anticipating the gods' return. Because of their prolonged absence from the world, any honor given them has been "invisible for too long." Yet poetic celebration of the gods is still crucial to us: "for every one of the heavenly ones demands sacrifice; but whenever one was neglected it has never brought anything good." The poem's concluding lines specify the exact type of divine service required at present:

> Wir haben gedienet der Mutter Erd'
> Und haben jüngst dem Sonnenlichte gedient,
> Unwissend, der Vater aber liebt,
> Der über allen waltet,
> Am meisten, dass gepfleget werde
> Der feste Buchstab, und Bestehendes gut
> Gedeutet. Dem folgt deutscher Gesang. (2:172)

(We have served our Mother Earth and lately have served the sunlight, unknowingly, but the Father who rules over all loves most that the fixed letter be cultivated and that which exists be well interpreted. Him German song obeys.)

As already stated in the fragmentary hymn "Der Mutter Erde," we must now attend to Mother Earth as the only locus of divine life known to us. We have also served the "sunlight" (another of Empedokles' elemental gods), perhaps through the enlightenment's devotion to truth. Yet the Father most especially wills that during this time of waiting we should studiously "cultivate" the "fixed letter" of sacred texts—the Bible, but possibly all literature devoted to the gods. Moreover, not only written texts but "whatever exists" ("Bestehendes") requires our interpretation. The deeds of the world have themselves functioned as commentaries upon obscure Scriptural prophecies, which in turn serve to illuminate the events themselves. The task of poetry is to elucidate (and further interpret) this dialectic of mutual interpretation. If poets better understand the divine significance of the historical process, they may, through proclaiming this significance, facilitate the optimal conclusion of the process; such service is the Father's mandate to "German song." The present hymn has provided an example of such service by offering elucidations both of Scripture (particularly John's Gospel and his Book of Revelations) and of the history of the world since Christ. The poet has thus benefited from his visionary visit to Patmos. By emulating St. John, he has been able to interpret John's writings in the light of world events up to the present. He thus ultimately returns "most loyal in spirit" to his own peak of time in order there to comply with the Father's will regarding the duty of present-day German poets.

Only three additional hymns were completed after "Patmos," which itself was subjected to a series of increasingly fragmentary revisions. "Andenken," "Der Ister," and "Mnemosyne" in its various versions are all characterized by a predominance of seemingly compulsive images which can be elucidated only with reference to similar imagery in Hölderlin's other writings. These poems are sometimes deficient in explicit conceptual content and thus often appear to lack any argument susceptible to paraphrase. Although appealing and highly evocative, they seem to defy linear interpretation. Thus any discussion of them must focus largely on the interplay of themes and motifs suggested by their imagistic patterns.

At first reading, the hymn "Andenken," dedicated to the "Remembrance" of his stay in Bordeaux, may seem merely a series of brilliantly evocative images with little or no coherence. The first stanza begins:

> Der Nordost wehet,
> Der Liebste unter der Winden
> Mir, weil er feurigen Geist
> Und gute Fahrt verheisset den Schiffern. (2: 188)

(The northeast is blowing, to me the most beloved of the winds because it promises fiery spirit and good voyage to the sailors.)

The speaker then bids the wind to visit the Garonne River and "the gardens of Bordeaux." There follows a description of a particular scene of a brook emptying into the river, while a "noble pair of oaks and silver poplars" look on. He then recalls other scenes: an elm forest around a mill and a fig tree growing in a courtyard, where "on holidays . . . brown women walked on silken ground:"

> Zur Märzenzeit,
> Wenn gleich ist Nacht und Tag,
> Und über langsamen Stegen,
> Von goldenen Träumen schwer,
> Einwiegende Lüfte ziehen. (2: 188)

(At the time in March when night and day are equal, and over slow paths, laden with golden dreams, lulling breezes move.)

Turning from these memories, the poet then observes that someone is now handing him "cup full of the dark light . . . so that I might sleep." For, he declares, "sweet would be the slumber amidst shadows." Yet (he remarks) it is also good to converse and to "hear much of days of love and deeds that occur."

At this point, we might stop to consider the possible thematic significance of some of the details in the poem. In his interpretation of the hymn, Jochen Schmidt observes that the "love" and heroic "deeds" mentioned in the third stanza constitute two principal themes.[8] Thus, he declares, the oaks and poplars in the first stanza are traditional emblems of heroism, whereas the second stanza's fig tree is emblematic of love, as are the alluring brown women and the feast days on which communal feelings are celebrated.[9] Another theme that might be observed in these stanzas is that of the appeal of oblivion: the brook emptying into the river, the breezes lulling to golden dreams, and of course the cup full of dark light, perhaps to be understood biographically as a narcotic sedative being offered to the ailing poet.

The heroic theme dominates the entire fourth stanza. The speaker seems to realize that the possibilities for such conversations as mentioned in the third stanza are now practically absent, for he is virtually alone. "Where," he asks, are his "friends"? As instances of friendship he cites "Bellarmin" and his "companion," presumably the Hyperion of the novel. They are here envisioned as having embarked on nautical adventures. (It should be recalled that Hyperion and Alabanda had for a while served in the Russian navy and participated in a sea battle.) "Some are reticent to go to the source; wealth namely begins in the sea." Just as "painters" assimilate various aspects of human or natural beauty to depict ideally beautiful persons or landscapes, so sailors facilitate the exchange (and ultimately the accumulation) of beautiful things. Moreover (as Schmidt points out), sailors become ideal embodiments of heroism in several of Hölderlin's late fragmentary poems. They in effect seek to unify a world whose parts would otherwise have no contact with one another.[10] But this heroic endeavor may often involve warlike struggles and condemn its participants to lives of austere loneliness; for the sailors must forego the joys of bacchanalian festivals such as the "holidays" recalled in the second stanza. The nocturnal comforts proclaimed in "Brot und Wein" and other poems are unavailable to those who choose the heroic life of the sea.

The poem's final stanza brings its various themes to resolution. The sailors have now set out on a voyage eastward to "the Indians," embarking from Bordeaux harbor, passing through the confluence of the Dordogne and the Garonne, and reaching the open sea at a promontory where the estuary has itself become "wide as the sea." As an attempt to attain rapport with a far distant part of the world, a passage to India might here signify an attempt (as in "Patmos") to reconcile the temporal peak of ancient Hindu culture with that of modern Europe. Such a meaning is merely suggested here, however. The poet is ostensibly less concerned with the sailors' distant goal than with the course of their departure. While the sailors' voyage is in keeping with the theme of heroism, the emptying of the rivers into the sea is here, as in many other poems, emblematic of individual dissolution into the all, the chosen destiny of Empedokles.

The final lines recapitulate the themes of the poem and suggest a resolution beyond their dialectic:

> Es nehmet aber
> Und gibt Gedächtnis die See
> Und die Lieb' auch heftet fleissig die Augen,
> Was bleibet aber, stiften die Dichter. (2:189)

(But the sea takes and gives memory, and love diligently fastens the eyes, but the poets establish that which remains.)

"Gedächtnis" here perhaps designates, more than ordinary memory, the power of holding in coherence all the data of experience, the unifying power of consciousness itself. Such cohesive memory is taken away by the sea as a symbol of dissolution, but it can also be enhanced or "given" by the sea as highway for the sailors whose heroic work of gathering is emblematic of the struggle for psychic unity.[11] And "love" in all its forms is the force that, by energetically arresting our gaze, would most strongly hold us to life in the present, thus checking the impulses both toward heroic endeavor and toward dissolution. Subjectively confronted with the impasse brought about by the conflict of these three tendencies, the poet surmounts it through triumphant affirmation of the full objective significance of his poetic vocation.

The poem's concluding line is one of the most famous in all of Hölderlin's poetry, and it has been subjected to a great variety of interpretations. One possible reading (for which I am again indebted to Jochen Schmidt) would view it in light of the ancient topos that only the poet can confer immortality on heroic deeds or on objects (or feelings) of love.[12] The sea, apart from symbolizing dissolution, can also, for Hölderlin, represent the transience or mutability of such things as love or heroism. In "Der Archipelagus," we recall, Hölderlin had spoken of the "language" of its waves as "Wechsel" and "Werden" ("change" and "becoming"). Against dissolution and transience, the poet affirms the power of poetic creation, which establishes permanence. Enduring beyond all moments of love or deeds of heroism, a poem will preserve and enshrine such transient things long after the dissolution of the poet's individuality in death—or in madness. Although seemingly mysterious, the concluding line thus asserts a truism that is entirely conventional, even a cliché. But it is a truism here invested with new significance by the thematic context of the poem it resolves.

"Der Ister" is probably the most opaque of Hölderlin's completed hymns. Its difficulty is of a different order than that of such poems as "Friedensfeier" or "Patmos," for a conceptual armature is almost totally lacking here. The poet does not, as in other hymns, offer interpretations, or even hints as to the interpretations, of his own symbols. The symbolic import of the images can only be inferred through analogy with the symbolic functions the images may possess in other late poems. As the functions of the images in other poems are themselves often problematic, any interpretation of this poem would be tentative at best. Thus, I will merely indicate the thematic contents of the poem's four sections.

"Ister" is the Latin name for the Danube. The hymn is thus another of Hölderlin's river poems, and we may perhaps assume that here, as in "Der Rhein" and elsewhere, a river represents an exemplary destiny. However, whereas in other poems the poet usually comments explicitly on the river's significance, he here offers only a few enigmatic remarks that serve primarily to contrast the Ister with the Rhine.

It may be possible to identify the speaker of the poem as a symbolic eagle (a messenger of Zeus) who, as in "Germanien" may be underway from the Orient—"vom Indus her / . . . und / vom Alpheus" (2:190)—to proclaim a divine epiphany to the Germans:

> Jetzt komme, Feuer!
> Begierig sind wir
> Zu schauen den Tag (2:190)

(Now come, fire! We are eager to behold the day.)

("Fire" and "day" are both figures of divine presence.)[13] It appears, however, that the speaker desires to stop and dwell by the Danube in its Balkan portion, virtually halfway between Greece and Germany. The poem's second section praises the fertility of the river's shore, where vegetation grows with firelike vitality and the trees paradoxically offer "coolness" in their shade. In ancient days, such coolness served to attract another of Zeus's servants, Hercules, from the "hot isthmus" of Greece.

In the third and fourth sections of the poem, the speaker rather obscurely contrasts the course of the personified Ister with that of the Rhine. Whereas the Rhine, after first violently seeking to go east, resigned himself to a northwesterly course, the Ister, while ultimately moving east, at times (in the Balkans) almost "seems to go backwards," so that he appears "to come from the east." The speaker remarks, "Vieles wäre / zu sagen davon" (2:191) ("there would be much to say about this"), but he does not elaborate. He later declares that the Ister seems to be "all too patient" ("allzugedultig") and to have an almost cynical attitude toward its fate: "und fast zu spotten" ("and almost to mock"). Whereas in his youth the Rhine had shown the free and fiery spirit of an untamed horse, the Ister in its upper course was listless and merely "satisfied" ("zufrieden") with his eastward (regressive) destiny. The poem ends with an expression of the speaker's own bafflement over the river: "Was aber jener tuet der Strom / Weiss niemand" (2:192) ("But what that one, the stream, is doing, nobody knows").

"Mnemosyne" was probably the last of Hölderlin's hymns to be completed.[14] As reconstructed by Friedrich Beissner, it exists in three versions differing chiefly in their opening stanzas. In the following brief discussion of the hymn's third version (which is nearly as obscure as "Der Ister"), I will again seek to trace the thematic development.

The poem's extremely dense first stanza is concerned, as was the first section of "Der Ister," with the question of "fire," divine life in its most intense and potentially destructive form. As Jochen Schmidt points out in his interpretation of the poem, this preoccupation with the threat of fiery immolation is reminiscent of Hölderlin's Empedokles dramas.[15] Thus, the process of ripening in the natural world is here depicted as a "cooking" process, and it is seen as a divine "law" that all things must ultimately pass away like smoke into the clouds, the "hills of heaven" ("Den Hügeln des Himmels" [2:197]). Schmidt observes that this heaven is to be understood as the realm of the Empedoklean "aorgisch," undifferentiated immediacy.[16] The natural elements themselves are viewed as about to go berserk from the indwelling fiery intensity of divine life. Against such a threat of universal dissolution, we as rational, conscious beings must make every exertion to hold together, to "maintain like a load of logs on our shoulders," the many things that constitute the contents of our minds and psyches. Yet, despite our efforts to make our world cohere, we also feel the temptation to abandon ourselves and

our burdensome consciousness to fiery immediacy: "And always a yearning goes into the unbounded" (Und immer / Ins Ungebundene gehet
eine Sehnsucht"). We need to resist this temptation, for "loyalty" to
psychic coherence is "needed." Yet, the stanza concludes, we long to live
purely in the present moment:

> Vorwärts aber und rückwarts wollen wir
> Nicht sehn. Uns wiegen lassen, wie
> Auf schwankem Kahne der See. (2:197)

(But we do not wish to look forward and backwards. Let ourselves be rocked, as
on the unsteady boat of the sea.)

This expression of the desire for tranquillity is followed, at the beginning
of the second stanza, by the description of a peaceful rustic setting
wherein such desires might be fulfilled. The tranquil "signs of day" in
this idyllic scene might be especially beneficial for someone whose "soul"
had been "wounded" by a god ("ein Himmlisches")—a possible reference to the painful psychic experience of 1802 described by the poet in
his first letter to Böhlendorff, where, we recall, it was said that he had
been as if "struck by Apollo." The latter part of this stanza modulates to
the description of an Alpine landscape whose green meadows partially
gleaming with snow may represent another "sign of day." Against this
background, the poet visualizes a "wanderer" ("Wandersmann") on a
"high road" apparently seeking to cross the Alps and "surmising afar"
(Fern ahnend") the distant goal of his journey.

The poem's third stanza indicates the journey's possible goal. It is the
world of ancient Greece, the goal of so many of the poet's spiritual
pilgrimages. It is not, however, the joyously festive Greece of "Brot und
Wein" or the intensely brilliant world of "Der Einzige" or "Patmos." It
is, instead, now perceived as a world permeated by death and steeped in
mourning. This stanza recalls the deaths of three of the warriors of the
Iliad. Ajax died because he yielded his soul to the forces of irrational
passion and psychic dissolution, going insane. Patroclos died resolutely
in the field of battle, wearing the armor of his royal friend Achilles ("in
des Königes Harnisch" [2:198]). Achilles' return to combat, which
made his early demise inevitable, was prompted by anguished and
furious mourning for the dead Patroklos. The stanza's conclusion is a
generalization about these modes of death:

Himmlische nämlich sind
Unwillig, wenn einer nicht die Seele schonend sich
Zusammengenommen, aber er muss doch; dem
Gleich fehlet die Trauer. (2:198)

(For the Heavenly Ones are displeased if someone does not pull himself together, thereby sparing his soul, but yet he must; likewise mourning is at fault.)

We must die regardless of whether we pull ourselves together to face our destiny (as did Patroklos), yield to the necessity of madness, both compelled by the gods and angering them (as did Ajax), or sin by the equally irrational fury of uncontrolled "mourning" (as did Achilles). If we refer these generalizations to the speaker's own situation as described in the first stanza, we can see how hopeless his predicament now appears to be. Whether he struggles to maintain mental and psychic balance or yields either to the dissolution of the irrational or to the kindred dissolution of unfettered mourning over his situation, the same tragic end awaits him. But this stanza provides yet another motive for a poet's mourning, for it proclaims the death in ancient times also of Mnemosyne, the mother of the muses. As Mnemosyne means "memory," mental coherence, which alone makes all art possible, her death (now fully realized) means the demise both of the poet's mastery of his own mind and of poetry in general.[18] If memory is now dead, we can no longer retrieve the past or make its heroes live again in poetry. The triumphant resolution at the end of "Andenken" is thus invalidated. This poem, which appropriately ends with the word "Trauer," announces the end of the poet's hopes and of his poetic capability. It is thus appropriately the last of Hölderlin's completed hymns.

Hölderlin also left behind, however, a fairly large number of uncompleted hymns and fragments in the hymnic style. Because of the extremely fragmentary nature of these verses as well as their cryptic phraseology, they are in most cases impossible to interpret as poems. The poet, in most cases, did not write, or supply, enough connective material to justify any interpreter's attempt to impose coherence upon them. Nevertheless, these writings contain isolated patches of fine poetry, and they are intriguing and generally important to scholars because of obvious conceptual or imagistic relationships between them and the completed poems. They can thus be, and have been, used as a kind of poetic quarry from which to mine parallels to assist in the interpretation of these poems.[19]

Also, a number of critics have undertaken thematic studies of some of the longer of the fragmentary hymns.[20] In many of these—such as "An die Madonna" (2:211–16), "Die Titanen" (2:217–19), "Wenn aber die Himmlischen . . ." (2:222–25), and "Griechenland" (2:254–58)— themes such as the absence of safely mediated divinity, the threat of consumption by the fire present in the growth of things, and the possibility of angry retribution from a yet distant divine being if our world succumbs to excessive violence are familiar from the later hymns. Other fragments seem to offer symbolic meditations on aspects of history ("Der Vatikan" [2:252–53]), or geography ("Das Nächste Beste" [2:233–39]), or on both history and geography ("Kolomb" [2:242– 45]). In general, it may be said that these fragments are of great interest and justify further attempts to specify and elucidate their imagistic and thematic structures.

There remain to be mentioned a small number of completed poems probably written at the time of the late hymns. Because they belong to no recognizable genre, Beissner has seen fit to categorize them as "individual forms."[21] One of them, "Lebensalter," laments (like the third stanza of "Mnemosyne") the death of the ancient world. It ends on a familiar note of mourning for its lost gods ("der Seligen Geister"). The most famous of them, however, is one of the best known of Hölderlin's poems, "Hälfte des Lebens." Its beautiful first stanza has won the admiration of nearly all readers and has been subjected to countless interpretations:

> Mit gelben Birnen hänget
> Und voll mit wilden Rosen
> Das Land in den See,
> Ihr holden Schwäne,
> Und trunken von Küssen
> Tunkt ihr das Haupt
> Ins heilignüchterne Wasser. (2:117)

(With yellow pears and full of wild roses the land hangs into the lake, you noble swans, and drunken with kisses you dunk your heads into the holy-sober water.)

I shall not attempt a full interpretation of the poem. It should be pointed out, however, that its title may refer to the poet's age at the time of composition. If he were then in his mid-thirties, he would be at the middle point of the traditional lifespan of seventy years. The first stanza, then, may be thought to articulate a happy man's wish that the second half of his life might repeat—or mirror—the beautiful fruition that he has now attained. The swan is traditionally an image of the soul, and these swans may represent a happily married couple optimistically looking into (or beyond) a looking-glass lake into their anticipated future of holy sobriety and continued prosperity and joy. The disquieting second stanza of the poem, then, may refer to the poet's own radically different anticipation of the future as a winter of alienation, human coldness, and the horrors of insanity.

The numerous short poems written during Hölderlin's actual period of insanity pose special problems to all readers. At first sight, they seem to be the work of a person completely different from the author of the late hymns. Whereas the hymns are syntactically, stylistically, and intellectually complex, these poems appear almost childish in the extreme simplicity of their syntax, style, and thought. They are written, for the most part, in rhymed quatrains, and the general predictability of their meter gives them often the appearance of doggerel. Yet the poems are not easy to read. While many of the later hymnic fragments appear beyond logic in their symbolic complexity, many of these poems seem sublogical in their seemingly artless incoherence. Yet, as has often been observed, the poems frequently contain passages notable for their freshness of observation and expression. It may be noted that few of Hölderlin's many interpreters have ventured detailed explications of any of these poems.[22]

Many of these poems appear to be meditations on the seasons of the year, almost in the tradition of mid-eighteenth-century moralizing poetry. Thus, of the forty-eight poems included under the heading "Späteste Gedichte" in the second volume of the *Stuttgarter Ausgabe,* nine are entitled "Der Frühling," five "Der Sommer," two "Der Herbst," and ten either "Winter" or "Der Winter." Most of these poems describe or allude to scenes characteristic of their respective seasons and express the poet's response to them. A number of the poems speak of how mankind in general ("Der Mensch" or "Die Menschheit") responds to the seasons. Thus, one of the "summer" poems declares, "der Menschen Leben / Es zeiget sich auf Meeren unverborgen" (2:285) (The life of men, it shows itself unhidden on seas); and one of the "spring" poems states, "Von Freuden ist die Menschheit sanft durchdrungen" (2:286) (Mankind is gently permeated by joys), while another declares, "Der Menschen Tätigkeit beginnt mit neuem Ziele" (2:288) (The activity of men begins with new goals). Other poems (like some of Hölderlin's earliest verse) are devoted to abstract topics: "Freundschaft, Liebe" (2:261), "Der Ruhm" (2:265), "Höhere Menschheit" (2:290), and "Der Mensch" (2:302). Many are signed "Scardanelli" (a name also used in Hölderlin's later letters) and are given fantastic dates, such as "Den 24. März 1671" (2:287) or "d. 9 ten Merz 1940" (2:297).

While some of these pieces seem virtually unreadable, others are quite moving, such as the following unrhymed poem:

> Nicht alle Tage nennet die schönsten der,
> > Der sich zurücksehnt unter die Freuden wo
> > > Ihn Freunde liebten wo die Menschen
> > > > Über dem Jüngling mit Gunst verweilten. (2:280)

(Not all days are called most beautiful by one who longs to be back among the joys where friends loved him [and] where people lingered over the youth with favor.)

Two poems are expressions of gratitude to Zimmer: one symbolically praises his skills as a carpenter—"Dädalus Geist und des Walds ist deiner" (2:271) (The spirit of Daedalus and of the forest is yours)—while the other (widely anthologized) develops an interesting simile:

> Die Linien des Lebens sind verschieden
> Wie Wege sind, und wie der Berge Grenzen.
> Was hier wir sind, kann dort ein Gott ergänzen
> Mit Harmonien und ewigem Lohn und Frieden. (2:268)

(The lines of life are diverse as paths are, and like the boundaries of mountains. What we are here, there a God can complete with harmonies and eternal reward and peace.)

Another poem often included in anthologies is "Der Spaziergang," which may record an actual recollection of one of the many walks that Hölderlin took in the company of Wilhelm Waiblinger. It has often been noted that there is an almost childlike freshness in the poem's evocation of aspects of the landscape:

> Ihr Wälder schön an der Seite,
> Am grünen Abhang gemalt,
> . . . .

> Ihr lieblichen Bilder im Tale,
> Zum Beispiel Gärten und Baum,
> Und dann der Steg der schmale,
> Der Bach zu sehen kaum,
> Wie schön aus heiterer Ferne
> Glänzt Einem das herrliche Bild
> Der Landschaft, die ich gerne
> Besuch' in Witterung mild. (2:276)

(You forests beautiful on the side, painted on the green slope . . . you lovely images in the valley, for example gardens and tree, and then the narrow path, the brook hardly to be seen; how beautiful from the bright distance there gleams for one the splendid image of the landscape which I like to visit when the weather is mild.)

It is regrettable that most of the poems written at the time of Hölderlin's insanity are not of comparable quality.

Chapter Nine
Hölderlin and His German Readers

During his long lifespan, Hölderlin was largely denied the recognition that he had once coveted and that the twentieth century has so amply bestowed upon him.[1] Goethe (who also failed to acknowledge the genius of Beethoven) had dismissed him as a talented eccentric, and, as already noted, Schiller (despite his earlier patronage) eventually came to share in this judgment. By 1806, when Hölderlin was transported to Tübingen, he had published only *Hyperion*, translations from Sophocles, and a fairly small number of poems. None of these publications had been greeted with much enthusiasm either by reviewers or by the reading public.

Historians of Hölderlin's reputation all note that the younger German romantics were the first group to ascribe real value to Hölderlin's poetry. Josef Görres, Clemens Brentano, and Achim von Arnim read with enthusiasm whatever of Hölderlin's work was available to them.[2] Alessandro Pellegrini observes that their lively interest in Hölderlin was to a large extent stimulated by Isaac von Sinclair, who proselytized for Hölderlin with almost religious zeal, depicting him as a prophet possessed by the deific spirit of "language" itself, mastered by its most fundamental rhythmic laws, and compelled almost against his will to articulate its spirit.[3] This view, which Sinclair promulgated among the romantics, was further elaborated by them and by later enthusiasts, leading eventually to what in this century has been termed the "Hölderlin myth."

Most of Hölderlin's poetic manuscripts were left in Sinclair's keeping, and after his death in 1815, they eventually passed into the hands of the Swabian poets Ludwig Uhland and Gustav Schwab, who, following the appearance of a new edition of *Hyperion* (1822), published the first collected edition of Hölderlin's poetry in 1826. The editors were highly selective. In a preface they announced that they were excluding both Hölderlin's earlier verse written under the influence of Schiller and those later poems in which (they felt) his mental disturbance was already apparent. A somewhat expanded edition, including the "Fragment von Hyperion" and a number of letters, was published by Christoph Theodor Schwab in 1846. No further editions were to appear until the end of the century.[4] Indeed, there was no demand for editions as the century progressed, for Hölderlin was almost universally ignored. The view persisted that he was an unstable sentimentalist consumed by nostalgia for ancient Greece—an opinion that, it must be admitted, would come readily to one who had given only superficial and unsympathetic attention to *Hyperion* and some of the elegiac poetry.[5] Perhaps the most prominent of Hölderlin's few admirers was Friedrich Nietzsche, who viewed him as a kindred spirit struggling like himself against the philistinism of bourgeois society. He regarded Hölderlin's Empedokles as a prototype for his own concept of the *Übermensch* and at one point had contemplated writing his own play on the Greek philosopher.[6]

Nietzsche's views on Hölderlin were eventually disseminated as his own work gained recognition. But of even greater influence on Hölderlin reception was Wilhelm Dilthey, who in his famous treatise *Das Erlebnis und die Dichtung* (1906) elaborated an interpretation of Hölderlin and his work that virtually established the image of Hölderlin that was most widely held in the early twentieth century. It is Dilthey's premise that our fundamental experience of life ("Erlebnis") is communicated most immediately—and thus most accurately—through art and especially through poetry. The true poet is thus a visionary ("ein Seher") who perceives the meaning of life, and (Dilthey declares) Hölderlin is the greatest of visionary poets. Because of the lucidity with which Hölderlin communicates the pure truth of experience, his work should be regarded virtually as inspired utterance.[7]

Of influence comparable to Dilthey's in enhancing Hölderlin's reputation was the poet Stefan George, who, with his disciples, dominated the German literary scene in the early part of this century. He not only admired the luminosity and stylistic rigor of Hölderlin's later poetry but also tended to accept at face value Hölderlin's implicit claim to be a prophet of the German future. A number of George's own poems proclaim his deep personal veneration of Hölderlin and his work.[8]

Even more directly responsible, however, for what can be called a Hölderlin renaissance was the historical-critical edition begun by the young George disciple Norbert von Hellingrath and continued (after his death on the battlefield in 1916) by Friedrich Seebass and Ludwig von Pigenot. The first volume appeared in 1913 and the sixth and final one was published in 1923.[9] It remained the standard edition until superseded by the *Grosse Stuttgarter Ausgabe.*

Hellingrath's edition of Hölderlin's late poems and fragments greatly stimulated the poet R. M. Rilke's interest in Hölderlin.[10] In his poem "An Hölderlin," Rilke expressed his almost religious adulation of the older poet.[11] It has been observed that the rigorous style of Hölderlin's late poetry was emulated by Rilke in some of his own later verse, such as the "Sonnets to Orpheus."[12] The prophetic tone of many of these poems and of the "Duino Elegies" may also be attributed in part to Hölderlin's influence. This influence can also be observed in the work of Georg Trakl, whose short life ended in the First World War. There are numerous allusions to Hölderlin and to his poetry in Trakl's verse.[13] Trakl has been associated with such German expressionist writers as Albert Ehrenstein and Georg Heym, and it can be argued that the influence of Hölderlin's ideas and style on this group was as pervasive as that exercised on the school of Stefan George.[14] It was, however, George and his disciples who generally set the tone for the German response to Hölderlin in the 1920s and who did the most to establish the image of Hölderlin most generally accepted during that decade.

This was again the image of a visionary prophet—but now a prophet of a rejuvenated and triumphant Germany.[15] The nationalistic element in Hölderlin's poetry—always linked with desires for a world where peace and democratic ideals would prevail—because almost absolute for many readers whose own patriotic feelings had been hurt by the war and the Treaty of Versailles. Hölderlin's always progressive nationalism was thus misinterpreted by most of the reading public and even by a number of prominent scholars, to accord with a resentful and generally reactionary national chauvinism. It was thus only a natural extension of this tendency that, after the Nazi takeover, Hölderlin was officially presented as a proto-fascist and (like Nietzsche) an inspired prophet of Hitler's *Volksgemeinschaft.*

Not all critical studies of these decades, however, were tainted by such chauvinism. Most critics at least sought scholarly objectivity, whatever their personal beliefs. Some, such as Frank Zinkernagel, editor of a Hölderlin edition meant to compete with that begun by Hellingrath, actually sought to discourage the view of Hölderlin as prophet.[16] It must be admitted, however, that most studies of Hölderlin written between the wars were characterized by a veneration bordering on adulation. Some who did not regard him as a prophet primarily of German greatness still extolled him as a "seer" capable of articulating the most exalted and recondite of truths. The philosopher Martin Heidegger esteemed Hölderlin as a poet whose works most fully articulate the "essence of poetry," and who was thus the greatest of modern poets.[17] Other studies dating from these decades, however, are less notable for their ideological tendencies than for their endeavors to determine Hölderlin's exact position in relation to the thought of his own time.[18] One highly influential study, Paul Böckmann's *Hölderlin und seine Götter*, elaborates on Hölderlin's celebration of irrational or demonic forces present in his experience of life, while others sought to specify Hölderlin's religious position and attitudes in distinction to those of orthodox Christianity.[19]

In addition to the nationalistic, metaphysical, or purely academic responses to Hölderlin's work in the years before the Second World War, we might also consider some of the responses on the part of those to the left of center of German politics or ideology. In her study *Hölderlin and the Left*, Helen Fehervary remarks that during the years of the Weimar Republic two general phases could be defined.[20] In the first phase, immediately after the war, many leftists viewed Hölderlin as a kindred spirit who anticipated their own detestation of war, authoritarianism, and bourgeois culture. The later Weimar years, however, were marked by growing Marxist orthodoxy among the dissidents and a concomitant tendency to dismiss Hölderlin along with Goethe, Schiller, and others venerated by the cultural establishment. It was felt that all these writers were too strongly representative of bourgeois values.[21] After the Nazis assumed power in 1933, however, Marxist writers who had been forced into exile felt compelled to reconsider their evaluations of German poets in the "bourgeois" tradition.[22] These writers assembled at the Congress of Soviet Writers in 1934 decided to challenge the Nazis' claims to be the heirs of everything valuable in the German cultural tradition. Most agreed that Hölderlin was the most progressive writer of what they considered the humanist tradition, because of his enthusiastic support for the French Revolution and continuing adherence to utopian ideals. It was argued that Hölderlin's "classical" ideal of perfected cultural harmony was essentially identical with the Marxists' own goals.[23]

Probably the most important—and certainly the most influential—prewar Marxist interpretation of Hölderlin was Georg Lukacs's 1935 essay "Hölderlin's *Hyperion*," representing him as a poet whose personal tragedy reflected the collective tragedy of the most noble of the revolutionary bourgeoisie.[24] As Fehervary points out, Lukacs's interpretation had a strong influence on subsequent Marxist criticism and formed the basis of the still prevailing view of Hölderlin in East Germany.[25] Also influenced by Lukacs was the poet Johannes R. Becher, who repeatedly celebrated Hölderlin's humanistic idealism in his own poetry. After the war, Becher established himself as East Germany's principal poet and a spokesman for the view that Hölderlin's dream of a perfect society had been realized in the German Democratic Republic.[26]

Hölderlin's chief promoter in Nazi Germany was Josef Weinheber, who, as one critic remarks, was considered by many of his fellow countrymen to be "Hölderlin's twentieth-century reincarnation."[27] During the war the spirit of Hölderlin was invoked by both sides. Becher, writing in exile, declared that the "heroes" of the struggle on the allied side should "bear also Hölderlin's name on their banners."[28] The Nazis, of course, exploited to the full Hölderlin's more militant poetry, such as "Der Tod fürs Vaterland," which had been written as an *anti*authoritarian poem. A number of "Hölderlin Breviaries" were compiled and issued to members of the *Wehrmacht*.[29] The year 1943 was proclaimed a "Hölderlin year" and the poet was celebrated and invoked as one whose spirit would lead the fatherland to victory. As remarked earlier, the founding of the *Hölderlin-Gesellschaft* that year was marked by a ceremony attended by Josef Goebbels. Yet, paradoxically, 1943 was also an important year in the history of serious Hölderlin scholarship. It saw the appearance of the first volume of the *Grosse Stuttgarter Ausgabe,* which, now complete, remains the standard edition. Despite its inauspicious beginnings, the *Hölderlin-Gesellschaft* survived the war and today remains the most important forum for discussion of Hölderlin's work in Germany.

In her analysis of the history of Hölderlin reception in postwar East Germany, Fehervary perceives two phases. In the earlier phase (1945–70), Hölderlin was predominantly and officially regarded as "the poet of harmony whose utopian vision would be realized" in the German socialist state.[30] This view of Hölderlin was, according to Fehervary, based on the interpretations of Lukacs and Becher.[31] She notes that this emphasis on Hölderlin as a harmonious poet led most East German critics to ignore the problems posed by his insanity.[32] In the later phase (since 1970), Fehervary observes both a tendency among major critics to dissent somewhat from the old "official" interpretation and, more important, a tendency on the part of creative writers to project images of Hölderlin not as a harmonious classical poet but as a historical individual suffering from alienation and from inner and outer conflicts.[33] Some writers even concentrate on the previously avoided topic of Hölderlin's madness; both Stephan Hermlin's radio play *Scardanelli* (1970) and Gerhard Wolf's novel *Der arme Hölderlin* deal with this problem.[34]

In West Germany, Fehervary notes, the response to Hölderlin on the part of most creative writers was at first quite different.[35] Here they generally felt aversion not only for the Nazi interpretation of Hölderlin but for the poet himself, who was deemed too filled with the high ideals and noble sentiments that the Nazis had so successfully exploited during the war. "Gruppe 47," which dominated the German literary scene during these years, thus rejected Hölderlin along with most of the German literary tradition. Ingo Seidler points out that poetic references to Hölderlin were chiefly in the form of sardonic allusions or parodies of some of his more exalted verses.[36] Yet not all poets of this time regarded Hölderlin with scorn; for Paul Celan, for example, he was a poet of tragic alienation. And since the 1960s, many West German writers have, like their counterparts in the East, discovered that Hölderlin was a poet not only of alienation but of revolution.[37] This discovery (or rediscovery) was stimulated in part by the Hölderlin interpretations of the respected Marxist critic Theodor W. Adorno and also by Robert Minder and Pierre Bertaux, who, in addresses at annual conventions of the *Hölderlin-Gesellschaft*, sought to redirect attention to the poet's radicalism.[38] In his speech (and later in his book *Hölderlin und die französische Revolution*),[39] Bertaux argued that Hölderlin remained a "Jacobin" throughout his life and that much of his difficult later poetry could be decoded as revolutionary messages. While such assertions were (and are) highly questionable, they did serve to provoke a heated debate on Hölderlin's politics and to arouse new interest in Hölderlin among nonacademic intellectuals. Bertaux's theses prompted the dramatist Peter Weiss to write a play, *Hölderlin* (1971), which, as Fehervary remarks, was virtually a "dramatic adaptation" of Bertaux's book.[40] Peter Härtling's 1976 novel *Hölderlin: Ein Roman* is further evidence of the fascination Hölderlin continues to exert on contemporary German writers.[41]

I have no intention here of attempting to summarize postwar academic criticism of Hölderlin. The accumulated scholarship is so voluminous and complicated that it would require a book-length study to sort it out. It may be observed, however, that the first twenty years after the war were characterized by a large number of philosophical interpretations of Hölderlin akin to those of earlier decades, but also by an increased emphasis on textual studies. The major event of the 1950s was (as noted earlier) the discovery and publication of "Friedensfeier." The year 1960 marked the publication of Lawrence Ryan's *Hölderlin's Lehre vom Wechsel der Töne,* a book that has encouraged further attempts to elucidate Hölderlin's difficult theoretical writings.[42] The most sensational happenings of the later 1960s were the publication of the above mentioned studies by Minder and Bertaux and the furor they aroused. Bertaux's assertions were refuted by Adolf Beck, who in his 1968 essay "Hölderlin als Republikaner," points out that Hölderlin's sympathies had been not with the Jacobins but with the more moderate Girondists.[43] The controversy did much to stimulate investigations of the relationship between poetry and political beliefs in Hölderlin's work, and in the 1970s a number of interesting and important studies were devoted to that topic.[44]

Beissner and Beck's *Grosse Stuttgarter Ausgabe* was completed (thirty-four years after the appearance of its first volume) with the publication of the seventh volume in 1977. In 1975, however, there had appeared the introductory volume of a projected *Frankfurter Ausgabe* of Hölderlin's works, edited by D. E. Sattler. Published by the *Verlag Roter Stern* in Frankfurt am Main, this edition was intended eventually to supplant the now standard *Stuttgarter Ausgabe.* In the highly polemical introductory volume, the editor announced his unusual editorial procedure. Unlike the Beissner edition, which printed the "definitive" version or versions of each poem in one book and its variants in another, this edition would seek to reconstruct the process by which each poem came into being.[45] As might be expected, this volume produced considerable controversy. Since 1975 five volumes of the *Frankfurter Ausgabe* have appeared, each greeted by a wide range of evaluations.[46]

Aside from the continuing controversy over this edition, the world of Hölderlin scholarship has in recent years once again been upset by Pierre Bertaux, now propounding a new thesis. In his 1978 book *Friedrich Hölderlin,* he asserts that the poet was never *really* insane but was merely pretending to be mad for forty years.[47] Bertaux's new book, like his old one, is often quite stimulating, but once again the majority of Hölderlin scholars seem unconvinced by his arguments. And once again he has been refuted (this time with some acerbity) by Adolf Beck.[48] However, Bertaux's new book, like his old one, may be of use in raising fresh issues among Hölderlin scholars. Already at least one book-length study has appeared that, while it disagrees with Bertaux, focuses fresh attention on various problems associated with Hölderlin's madness.[49] We might, then, expect to see in the 1980s a number of studies dealing with biographical and psychological issues. The one virtual certainty is that academic and general interest in this poet—perhaps the greatest European poet of the last two hundred years—will continue to grow.

Notes and References

Preface

1. *Hölderlin Werke und Briefe,* ed. Friedrich Beissner and Jochen Schmidt, 2 vols. (Frankfurt am Main, 1968); hereafter cited as Beissner/Schmidt.
2. See Friedrich Hölderlin, *Sämtliche Werke. Grosse Stuttgartner Ausgabe,* ed. Friedrich Beissner and Adolf Beck, 7 vols. (Stuttgart, 1943–77), 6:413–14; hereafter cited as *GSA.*
3. Richard Unger, *Hölderlin's Major Poetry: The Dialectics of Unity* (Bloomington, Ind. 1975).

Chapter One

1. In preparing this chapter, I have relied extensively on the information presented in Adolf Beck and Paul Raabe, *Hölderlin. Eine Chronik in Text und Bild* (Frankfurt am Main, 1970) (hereafter cited as Beck), the most comprehensive listing of the chronological data of Hölderlin's life; and in Wilhelm Michel, *Das Leben Friedrich Hölderlins* (Bremen, 1940; reprint, Frankfurt am Main, 1967), which remains the best critical biography of the poet.
2. See Jean Laplanche, *Hölderlin et la question du père* (Paris, 1961).
3. On the subject of Pietistic influence on Hölderlin, see especially Peter H. Gaskill, "Christ and the Divine Economy in the Work of Friedrich Hölderlin" (Ph.D. dissertation, Cambridge University, 1971).
4. See Roy C. Shelton, *The Young Hölderlin* (Berne and Frankfurt am Main, 1973), pp. 21–35. Shelton offers a stimulating if unsympathetic (and often hostile) pathological analysis of the first twenty-five years of the poet's life.
5. See Michel, *Leben,* pp. 36–38.
6. See Beck, p. 22.
7. On the so-called Pantheismusstreit, see Max Bäumer, "Hölderlin und das *Hen Kai Pan,*" *Monatshefte für deutschen Unterricht* 59 (Summer 1967): 131–47. As will be observed in later chapters, the doctrine of pantheism plays a crucial role in Hölderlin's early thought and poetry.
8. See Shelton, *The Young Hölderlin,* p. 209.
9. See Michel, *Leben,* pp. 99–130; Shelton, *The Young Hölderlin,* pp. 240–79; Laplanche, *Hölderlin,* pp. 25–75. Hölderlin's distress at Jena may have been compounded if, as some evidence suggests, he was the father of an illegitimate child born that year.
10. On Hölderlin's relationship with Sinclair, see Michel, *Leben,* pp. 107–10.

11. For various speculations on the cause, see ibid., pp. 126–27; Shelton, *The Young Hölderlin,* pp. 276–79; Laplanche, *Hölderlin,* pp. 611–75.

12. See Michel, *Leben,* pp. 127–31.

13. Ibid., pp. 145–60.

14. Ibid., p. 229.

15. See Beck, p. 54.

16. Hölderlin's theoretical essays are extremely difficult to decipher, as they were apparently not designed for publication but represent the poet's struggle to articulate for himself, in a kind of conceptual code, his own highly complicated meditations on the inner dialectics of poetic forms and on the relationship of art to life. In the last several decades, a number of valiant attempts have been made to explicate these texts and to establish their relationship to Hölderlin's poetic practice. Major studies have included Lawrence Ryan, *Hölderlins Lehre vom Wechsel der Töne* (Stuttgart, 1960), Walter Hof, *Hölderlins Stil* (Meisenheim/ Glan, 1956), and Ulrich Gaier, *Der gesetzliche Kalkül* (Tübingen, 1962).

17. See Michel, *Leben,* pp. 304–5.

18. See Cyrus Hamlin, "Hölderlin's Elegy 'Homecoming': Comments," in *Friedrich Hölderlin: An Early Modern,* ed. Emery E. George (Ann Arbor, 1970), pp. 232–45.

19. *GSA,* 6:421–23.

20. Ibid., 6:424–28.

21. See Beck, p. 64.

22. *GSA,* 6:432–33.

23. See Beck, p. 64.

24. Ibid., p. 65. It has recently been suggested that Hölderlin may have been present at Susette's death in Frankfurt. Regarding this controversy, see two articles in the combined vols. 19–20 of the *Hölderlin Jahrbuch* (1975–77); Pierre Bertaux, "Hölderlin in und nach Bordeaux/Eine biographische Untersuchung," pp. 94–111, and Adolf Beck, "Hölderlin im Juni 1802 in Frankfurt? zur Frage seiner Rückkehr von Bordeaux," pp. 458–75.

25. *GSA,* 6:432–33.

26. On the basis of this letter, most German editors of Hölderlin's poetry (assuming that he is referring here to his own most recent poetry) have applied the categorical label "vaterländische Gesänge" to Hölderlin's Pindaric hymns.

27. *GSA,* vol. 7, pt. 2, p. 299.

28. For a detailed study of the accusations against Sinclair, their consequences, and the ensuing complications in Hölderlin's own life, see Werner Kirchner, *Der Hochverratsprozess gegen Sinclair* (Marburg am Lahn, 1949). See also *GSA,* vol. 7, pt. 2, pp. 317–20.

29. See Michel, *Leben,* p. 454.

30. A recent book by Pierre Bertaux, *Friedrich Hölderlin* (Frankfurt am Main: Suhrkamp, 1978), assembles all pertinent documents from the final period of the poet's life and, with great rhetorical verve and finesse, proceeds to argue on

the basis of this evidence that Hölderlin was never actually insane. This stimulating (if generally unconvincing) book has, of course, produced a great deal of controversy.

31. Waiblinger's book has been reprinted in an edition by Jochen Schmidt, *Dichter über Hölderlin* (Frankfurt am Main: Insel, 1969), pp. 5–51; the text also appears in *GSA,* vol. 7, pt. 3, pp. 50–80.

32. See "Bericht über die Veranstaltungen," in *Iduna: Jahrbuch der Hölderlin-Gesellschaft* 1 (1944):12. For a retrospective view of the occasion, see Theodor Pfizer, "Die Hölderlin-Gesellschaft: Anfänge und Gegenwart," *Hölderlin Jahrbuch* 21 (1978–79):23.

Chapter Two

1. Dating for this poem and other poems discussed in this and subsequent chapters is taken from *Friedrich Hölderlin: Sämtliche Gedichte,* ed. with commentary by Detlev Lüders, 2 vols. (Bad Homburg, 1970); hereafter cited in the notes as Lüders.

2. Ibid., 2:69–70.

3. Ibid., 2:74–76; see also Adolf Beck, "Hölderlins Hymne an den Genius Griechenlands," in *Überlieferung und Auftrag: Otto Heuschele zum 50. Geburtstag* (Stuttgart: J. F. Steinkopf, 1950), pp. 49–58.

4. See Michel, *Leben,* pp. 62–63. For a general discussion of the philosophical implications of these poems, see Wolfgang Binder, "Einführung in Hölderlin's Tübinger Hymnen," *Hölderlin-Jahrbuch* 18 (1973–74):1–19. For a recent appraisal of their political background, see Christoph Prignitz, "Hölderlins früher Patriotismus: Struktur und Wandlungen seines patriotischen Denkens bis zu den Tübinger Hymnen," *Hölderlin-Jahrbuch* 21 (1978–79):36–66.

5. See Friedrich Beissner, "Hölderlins Hymne an die Schönheit," in *Hölderlin* (Weimar, 1961), pp. 15–30.

6. See Lüders, 2:106–7.

7. See Ulrich Hötzer, *Die Gestalt des Herakles in Hölderlins Dichtung* (Stuttgart, 1956), pp. 42–47.

8. See Adolf Beck, "Hölderlin und Friedrich Leopold Graf zu Stolberg," *Iduna: Jahrbuch der Hölderlin-Gesellschaft* 1 (1944):88–114.

9. See Rudolf D. Schier, "Trees and Transcendence: Hölderlin's 'Die Eichbäume' and Rilke's 'Herbst,'" *German Life and Letters* (1966–67), pp. 331–41.

10. For a general discussion of Hölderlin's concept of "Aether," see Jochen Schmidt, *Hölderlins Elegie "Brod und Wein"* (Berlin, 1968), pp. 209–18.

11. Many philologists believe that some of the words for *god* in the Italic, Celtic, Baltic, and Indo-Iranian branches of the Indo-European language family are derived from a common root, meaning (probably) "heavenly one"; the Greek

name *Zeus* is likewise thought to be derived from this root. See C. D. Buck, *A Dictionary of Selected Synonyms in the Principal Indo-European Languages* (Chicago: University of Chicago Press, 1949), p. 1464.

12. See Lüders, 2:163.

Chapter Three

1. Lawrence Ryan, "Hölderlins *Hyperion:* Ein 'romantischer' Roman?" in *Über Hölderlin,* ed. Jochen Schmidt (Frankfurt am Main, 1970), pp. 175–212. This work eloquently demonstrates the intellectual complexity of the novel. Ryan's book, *Hölderlins "Hyperion": Exzentrische Bahn und Dichterberuf* (Stuttgart, 1965) remains one of the foremost studies of the novel. Friedbert Aspetsberger, *Welteinheit und epische Gestaltung: Studien zur Ichform von Hölderlins Roman Hyperion* (Munich, 1971) is another study of major importance. Walter Silz, *Hölderlin's Hyperion: A Critical Reading* (Philadelphia, 1969) is probably the most detailed study of the novel in English. For a complete analytical account of the novel's genesis, see Beissner/Schmidt, notes, 1:[161–75].

2. *GSA,* 3:163.

3. Among the studies dedicated to the problem of the "exzentrische Bahn," see, in addition to the above mentioned books by Ryan and Aspetsberger, Wolfgang Schadewaldt, "Das Bild der exzentrischen Bahn bei Hölderlin," *Hölderlin-Jahrbuch* 6 (1952):1–16.

4. *GSA,* 3:235–37.

5. See Beissner/Schmidt, notes 1:[172–75].

6. See Michel, *Leben,* pp. 118–36; Ryan, *Hölderlins Hyperion,* pp. 33–57.

7. This juxtaposition of "god" and "beggar" recalls Socrates' discourse on love in the *Symposium,* where love is described as a spirit begotten of the god Wealth on the beggar-woman Poverty. *The Symposium* should always be kept in mind while reading the novel.

8. See Jean Laplanche, *Hölderlin und die Suche nach dem Vater,* trans. H. K. Schnutz (Stuttgart-Bad Cannstadt: Frommann-Holzboog, 1975), pp. 93–96.

9. Many interpreters see strong similarities between the character of Alabanda and that of Isaac von Sinclair. See, for example, Michel, *Leben,* p. 109.

10. Hyperion's contrast of the present "ideal" to past reality ("nature") is probably derived from Schiller's essays *Über Anmut und Würde* and *Über naive und sentimentalische Dichtung.* See Beissner/Schmidt, notes, 1:184. It might also be noted that in this passage the development of mankind as a whole is presented as analogous to the development of the individual as expounded in the novel's preface.

11. See Aspetsberger, *Welteinheit und epische Gestaltung,* pp. 42–68.

12. One might compare the concept of inspiration here propounded by Hyperion with Coleridge's ideas on the imagination. See Coleridge's *Biographia*

Literaria, ed. John Shawcross (Oxford: Oxford University Press, 1907), 2:12.

13. This historical event occurred in 1770. On the significance of Hyperion's involvement in the rebellion, particularly apropos of Hölderlin's complicated and shifting attitudes toward the French Revolution, see Christoph Prignitz, *Friedrich Hölderlin: Die Entwicklung seines politischen Denkens unter dem Einfluss der Französischen Revolution* (Hamburg: Buske, 1976), pp. 140–226.

14. See, for example, Ryan, *Hölderlin's Hyperion,* pp. 212–28; Aspetsberger, *Welteinheit und epische Gestaltung,* pp. 82–148.

15. See Beissner/Schmidt, notes, 1:[194].

16. See Aspetsberger, *Welteinheit und epische Gestaltung,* pp. 132–48.

17. See Ryan, *Hölderlins Hyperion,* pp. 227–28.

Chapter Four

1. See Friedrich Hölderlin, *Der Tod des Empedokles,* ed. with an introduction by M. B. Benn (Oxford: Oxford University Press, 1968), p. 7. For more thorough accounts of the play's genesis, see Uvo Hölscher, *Empedokles und Hölderlin* (Frankfurt am Main, 1965), and Friedrich Beissner, "Hölderlins Trauerspiel *Der Tod des Empedokles* in seinen drei Fassungen," in *Hölderlin: Reden und Aufsätze* (Weimar, 1961).

2. See Benn, introduction, pp. 13–15. See also, Beissner/Schmidt, notes, 2:201–4.

3. *GSA,* 4:145–48.

4. At this point, the fragmentary character of this version asserts itself as lacunae begin to appear in the text, often in Empedokles' speeches. However, the gist of these speeches is still fairly clear.

5. See Beissner/Schmidt, notes, 2:212.

6. Ibid., notes, 2:211.

7. See Benn, introduction, p. 39. Benn suggests that Hölderlin may here be emulating the free verse of some of Goethe's hymns, such as "Prometheus" or "Ganymed."

8. For the fullest analysis of the problem of Empedokles' "justification" (in the theological sense), see Jürgen Söring, *Die Dialektik der Rechtfertigung: Überlegungen zu Hölderlins Empedokles-Projekt* (Frankfurt am Main, 1973).

9. *GSA,* 4:149–62. My analysis is indebted to Lawrence Ryan, *Friedrich Hölderlin,* 2d ed. (Stuttgart, 1967), pp. 50–51. Whereas the "Grund zum Empedokles" concentrates on the interaction between a civilization and its destroyer-redeemer, the essay "Das Werden im Vergehen," (*GSA,* 4:282–87), written at approximately the same time, is devoted to dialectical tensions and developments within the civilization in the process of being transformed.

10. *GSA,* 4:163–68.

11. See, for example, Ryan, *Friedrich Hölderlin,* pp. 59–60.

Chapter Five

1. For a general discussion of the metrics of the odes, see Wolfgang Binder, "Hölderlins Odenstrophe," in *Hölderlin-Aufsätze*, pp. 47–75.

2. The poet is referring perhaps to opportunists or fanatics such as Robespierre.

3. This idea is most fully developed in the hymns "Am Quell der Donau" and "Germanien."

4. See also the first stanza of "Germanien."

5. Hölderlin felt that Rousseau had been generally misunderstood by his interpreters. In the later hymn, "Der Rhein," Hölderlin would offer his own interpretation of Rousseau.

6. See Beissner/Schmidt, notes, 1:27–28. For a detailed explication of the poem, see Emil Staiger, "Hölderlins Ode 'Natur und Kunst oder Saturn und Jupiter,'" in *Über Hölderlin*, ed. Schmidt, pp. 33–44.

7. Lüders, p. 206, further points out that Hölderlin's concern for redressing the Art-Nature balance is evidenced also in his correspondence at the time of the poem's composition.

8. See Beissner/Schmidt, notes, 1:29–30.

9. See, for example, Friedrich Beissner, "Dichterberuf," in *Hölderlin* (Weimar, 1961), pp. 110–25; Guido Schmidlin, *Hölderlins Ode: "Dichterberuf": Eine Interpretation* (Berne: Francke, 1958).

10. See Beissner/Schmidt, notes, 1:31.

11. See Beissner/Schmidt, notes, 1:32. To Apollo is here attributed a function reserved in other poems for the "Zeitgeist" or for Zeus as "Herr der Zeit."

12. See Hans Pyritz, "Zum Fortgang der Stuttgarter Hölderlin-Ausgabe," *Hölderlin-Jahrbuch* (1953), pp. 80–105; Martin Heidegger, "Hölderlin und das Wesen der Dichtung," in *Erläuterungen zu Hölderlins Dichtung* (Frankfurt am Main: Klastermann, 1951), pp. 31–45.

13. See Beissner/Schmidt, notes, 1:34–35.

14. The Latin proverb is "Vox populi vox dei."

15. See Beissner/Schmidt, notes 1:35–36.

16. See Lüders, p. 219. For thorough and stimulating discussions of several of these poems (and their earlier versions), see Jochen Schmidt, *Hölderlins später Widerruf* (Tübingen, 1978).

17. Ibid., pp. 16–102.

18. On "Dichtermut" and "Blödigkeit," see Schmidt, *Hölderlins später Widerruf*, pp. 103–45; Walter Benjamin, "Zwei Gedichte von Friedrich Hölderlin," in *Über Hölderlin*, pp. 45–67.

19. See Schmidt, *Hölderlins später Wiederruf*, pp. 146–76.

Chapter Six

1. *Princeton Encyclopedia of Poetry and Poetics*, enl. ed., 1974, p. 215.

2. Ibid., p. 216. See Schiller, *Werke*, ed. Lieselotte Blumenthal and Benno von Wiese (Weimar: Hermann Böhlaus Nachfolger, 1962), 20:448–51. For a

detailed study of the formal aspects of Hölderlin's elegies, see Beissner, "Hölderlins Elegien," in *Über Hölderlin,* ed. Schmidt, pp. 68–86.

3. See Beissner/Schmidt, notes, 1:48.

4. On the special significance of Aether for Hölderlin, see Jochen Schmidt, *Hölderlins Elegie "Brot und Wein,"* pp. 100–104.

5. Ibid., pp. 8–10.

6. This problem is studied in depth in Momme Mommsen, "Dionysos in der Dichtung Hölderlins," *Germanisch-Romanische Monatsschrift* 13 (1963): 345–79, and in Max Bäumer, "Dionysos und das Dionysische bei Hölderlin," *Hölderlin-Jahrbuch* 18 (1973–74):105–11.

7. For a general discussion of the problems of All-Unity in Hölderlin's work, see my earlier book, *Hölderlin's Major Poetry: The Dialectics of Unity.*

8. See Beissner/Schmidt, notes 1:57–58.

9. Ibid., 1:58.

10. See Beissner's comments in *GSA,* 2:684. For a thorough analysis, see Jürg Peter Walser, *Hölderlins Archipelagus* (Zurich, 1962).

11. See Beissner/Schmidt, notes, 1:62.

12. Martin Heidegger, in *Erläuterungen,* pp. 9–30, reads the first stanza as a complex allegory of the process of poetic composition. Paul de Man, "The Intentional Structure of the Romantic Image," *Romanticism and Consciousness,* ed. Harold Bloom (New York, 1970), p. 75, noting the inordinately large number of oxymoric expressions in the stanza, concludes that, for Hölderlin, an experience of extreme contradictions in the objective world must precede an illumination of pure subjectivity (the religious vision in the second stanza).

13. See Cyrus Hamlin, "Hölderlin's Elegy 'Homecoming': Comments," in *Hölderlin,* ed. George, pp. 234–35.

Chapter Seven

1. For a more thorough discussion of the "Feiertag" hymn see Peter Szondi, *Hölderlin-Studien* (Frankfurt am Main, 1967), pp. 33–54.

2. This identification is established later in the stanza. See ibid., p. 37.

3. Ibid., p. 38.

4. Ibid., p. 45.

5. See Unger, *Hölderlin's Major Poetry,* pp. 119–22.

6. See *GSA,* 2:687.

7. See Beissner/Schmidt, notes, 1:72.

8. A similar pun occurs in the ode "Blödigkeit" (2:66).

9. The poet's wish as expressed in these lines can be interpreted in either of two ways. Either he desires that the present Germans might again visit and intermarry with the contemporary descendants of the children of the sun in order to produce another progeny comparable to the ancient Greeks or he perhaps wishes, as in other poems, to visit the modern descendants of the ancient Greeks.

10. See Beissner/Schmidt, notes, 1:78.

11. Ibid., 1:89.

12. Ibid.

13. Ibid., 1:89–90.

14. For a detailed general discussion of "Der Rhein," see Bernhard Böschenstein, *Hölderlins Rheinhymne* (Zurich and Freiburg in Breisgau, 1968). For a study of the poem's complex ideological implications, see Johannes Mahr, *Mythos und Politik in Hölderlins Rheinhymne* (Munich, 1972).

15. *GSA*, 2:722. For an interpretation of this note, see Böschenstein, *Hölderlins Rheinhymne*, pp. 152, 137–38. See also Lüders, 1:290–92.

16. See Michel, *Leben*, p. 368.

17. See Böschenstein, *Hölderlins Rheinhymne*, pp. 92–93. For a general discussion of Rousseau's significance for Hölderlin, see Paul de Man, "Hölderlins Rousseaubild," *Hölderlin-Jahrbuch* 15 (1967–68):180–208.

18. See Böschenstein, *Hölderlins Rheinhymne*, p. 196.

19. In the original version, the hymn concluded with a final stanza addressed to Wilhelm Heinse. See *GSA*, 2:729.

20. For a listing and analysis of the various interpretations of the poem up to 1960, see Alessandro Pellegrini, *Friedrich Hölderlin. Sein Bild in der Forschung* (Berlin, 1965), pp. 372–449. A more selective list of interpretations to 1965 is provided by Lawrence Ryan, *Friedrich Hölderlin*, 2d ed., p. 90.

21. See *GSA*, 3:534.

22. For a full list of conjectures as to the identity of the prince, see G. Schneider-Herrman, *Hölderlins "Friedensfeier" und der griechische Genius* (Zurich: Origo, 1959), pp. 83–85.

23. "Theilen alles Schicksal" could be interpreted as meaning either "share out [or distribute] all destiny" or "participate in all destiny."

24. I here prefer the reading "Zeichen, das" (relative pronoun) to Beissner's reading "Zeichen, dass" (conjunction), because the former seems to make more sense.

25. This is one of the most disputed passages in the poem. "Darum rief ich / . . . / . . . dich zum Fürsten des Festes" can be interpreted either as "call to [meet] the Prince" or as "call to [be] the Prince." Both readings are possible; the latter is preferred by those who identify the prince with Christ. I prefer the former reading because it seems more plausible in terms of the poem as a whole.

26. Cf. Matt. 2:25–32.

27. My reading here assumes that nature's "children" are to be understood as the gods. It is also possible (though probably less plausible) to understand them as men. See *GSA*, 3:567–68.

28. See Binder, *Hölderlin-Studien*, p. 155.

Chapter Eight

1. For interpretations of the poem, see Robert Thomas Stoll, *Hölderlins Christushymnen: Grundlagen und Darstellung* (Basel, 1952), pp. 151–84; Romano

Guardini, *Hölderlin: Weltbild und Frömmigkeit* (Munich: Kösel, 1955), pp. 520–30; and Unger, *Hölderlin's Major Poetry*, pp. 171–79.

2. See Stoll, *Hölderlin's Christushymnen*, p. 164.

3. For interpretations of "Patmos," see Binder, "Hölderlin's Patmos-Hymne," in *Hölderlin-Aufsätze*, pp. 262–403; Gaskill, "Christ and the Divine Economy in the Work of Friedrich Hölderlin" (Ph.D. dissertation, Cambridge University, 1971), pp. 39–84; Stoll, *Hölderlins Christushymnen*, pp. 184–239; and Unger, *Hölderlin's Major Poetry*, pp. 180–205.

4. See Werner Kirchner, *Hölderlin: Aufsätze zu seiner Homburger Zeit* (Göttingen, 1967), pp. 57–68.

5. See Böschenstein, *Hölderlins Rheinhymne*, pp. 7–11; Binder, *Hölderlin-Aufsätze*, p. 731; Schmidt, *Hölderlins Elegie "Brot und Wein,"* pp. 2–3; Guardini, *Hölderlin*, p. 523.

6. See Binder, *Hölderlin-Aufsätze*, p. 378.

7. Ibid.

8. See Jochen Schmidt, *Hölderlins letzte Hymnen* (Tübingen, 1970), pp. 1–49; see also Beissner/Schmidt, notes, 1:122–23.

9. Ibid., notes, 1:123.

10. Ibid., pp. 123–24.

11. Ibid., p. 124.

12. Ibid.

13. Ibid., pp. 125–26.

14. For my interpretation of "Mnemosyne," also, I am generally following Schmidt's interpretation; see *Hölderlins letzte Hymne*, pp. 50–80. See also Raymond Furness, "The Death of Memory: An Analysis of Hölderlin's Hymn Mnemosyne," *Publications of the English Goethe Society*, n.s. 40 (1970):38–68.

15. Schmidt, *Hölderlins letzte Hymnen*, pp. 71–73.

16. Ibid.

17. For a discussion of these lines (and for a fuller analysis of the entire poem), see Unger, *Hölderlin's Major Poetry*, pp. 206–20.

18. See Schmidt, *Hölderlins letzte Hymnen*, p. 68.

19. Such a method was used with great success by Bernhard Böschenstein in *Hölderlins Rheinhymne*. Böschenstein's compilation of a concordance of Hölderlin's later poetry (*Konkordanz zu Hölderlins Gedichten nach 1800* [Göttingen: Vandenhock & Ruprecht, 1964]) has been of considerable help to others who have also followed this procedure.

20. See Windfried Kudszus, *Sprachverlust und Sinnwandel: Zur späten und spätesten Lyrik Hölderlins* (Stuttgart, 1969), for discussions of "der Vatikan" (pp. 56–73) and "Griechenland" (pp. 74–131). For a discussion of "Die Titanen," see Arthur Häny, *Hölderlins Titanenmythos* (Zurich, 1948).

21. See *GSA*, 2:115–17.

22. There have, however, been a number of thematic studies of the poems; see Böschenstein, "Hölderlins späteste Gedichte," in *Über Hölderlin*, pp. 153–74; Kudszus, *Sprachverlust und Sinnwandel*, pp. 132–46.

Chapter Nine

1. In preparing this chapter, I am greatly indebted to previous historical surveys of Hölderlin's reception, particularly Lawrence Ryan's *Friedrich Hölderlin*, pp. 1–16; Pellegrini's *Friedrich Hölderlin;* Helen Fehervary's *Hölderlin and the Left: The Search for a Dialectic of Art and Life* (Heidelberg, 1977); and Bernhard Böschenstein's *Leuchttürme: Von Hölderlin zu Celan. Wirkung und Vergleich. Studien* (Frankfurt am Main: Insel, 1977), pp. 64–87. Werner Bartscher's *Hölderlin und die deutsche Nation: Versuch einer Wirkungsgeschichte* (Berlin: Junker & Dünnhaupt, 1942), though tainted with Nazism, is still useful on the nineteenth-century reception.

2. See Ryan, *Friedrich Hölderlin*, p. 1.

3. Pellegrini, *Friedrich Hölderlin*, pp. 21–26.

4. Ibid., pp. 26–27; see also Ryan, *Friedrich Hölderlin*, p. 2.

5. See Ryan, *Friedrich Hölderlin*, p. 3.

6. See Pellegrini, *Friedrich Hölderlin*, pp. 39–40; Ryan, *Friedrich Hölderlin*, p. 3.

7. Wilhelm Dilthey, *Gesammelte Schriften* (Stuttgart and Göttingen: Teubner, 1959), 5, 274; 5, 394. See Pellegrini, *Friedrich Hölderlin*, pp. 40–43; Fehervary, *Hölderlin and the Left*, pp. 19–23.

8. See Hermann Pongs, "Einwirkung Hölderlins auf die deutsche Dichtung seit der Jahrhundertwende," *Iduna: Journal der Hölderlin-Gesellschaft* 1 (1944): 129–32.

9. *Sämtliche Werke: Historisch-kritische Ausgabe* (Munich and Leipzig: G. Müller, 1913–23).

10. See Pongs, "Einwirkung Hölderlins," pp. 142–43; Böschenstein, *Leuchttürme*, pp. 65–67; see also Ingo Seidler, " 'Stifter einer weiteren Ahnenreihe?' Hölderlin's Influence on German Poets of the Twentieth Century," in *Friedrich Hölderlin: An Early Modern*, pp. 64–86.

11. Rilke, *Werke in drei Bänden* (Frankfurt am Main: Insel, 1966), 2:93–94.

12. See Böschenstein, *Leuchttürme*, pp. 67–71: Seidler, " 'Stifter einer weiteren Ahnenreihe?' " pp. 70–73; Pongs, "Einwirkung Hölderlins," pp. 143–48.

13. See Böschenstein, *Leuchtturme*, pp. 71–76.

14. See Kurt Barsch, *Die Hölderlin-Rezeption im deutschen Expressionismus* (Frankfurt am Main: Akademische Verlagsgesellschaft, 1974), pp. 1–7. Barsch analyzes in some detail the influence of Hölderlin on Trakl's style, as does Theodore Fiedler, "Hölderlin and Trakl's Poetry of 1914," in *Friedrich Hölderlin: An Early Modern*, pp. 87–105.

15. See Böschenstein, *Leuchttürme*, pp. 64–67; Fehervary, *Hölderlin and the Left*, pp. 23–26.

16. See Franz Zinkernagel, ed., *Friedrich Hölderlin, Sämtliche Werke und Briefe*, 5 vols. (Leipzig: Insel, 1923–26).

17. See *Erläuterungen zu Hölderlins Dichtung* (Frankfurt am Main, 1951).

18. See Wilhelm Böhm, *Hölderlin*, 2 vols. (Halle: Niemeyer, 1928–30); H. A. Korff, *Geist der Goethezeit*, 4 vols. (Leipzig: Herzel, 1923–57); Ernst Müller,

Hölderlin: Studien zur Geschichte seines Geistes (Stuttgart and Berlin, 1944); Johannes Hoffmeister, *Hölderlin und die Philosophie*, 2d ed. (Leipzig, 1944).

19. Paul Böckmann, *Hölderlin und seine Götter* (Munich, 1935); Guardini, *Hölderlin.*

20. See Fehervary, *Hölderlin and the Left*, p. 33.

21. Ibid., p. 38.

22. Ibid., pp. 42–51.

23. Ibid., p. 44.

24. Georg Lukacs, "Hölderlin's *Hyperion*," *Internationale Literatur*, June 1935, pp. 96–110. See Fehervary, *Hölderlin and the Left*, pp. 59–65.

25. See Fehervary, *Hölderlin and the Left*, p. 108.

26. Ibid., pp. 76–79, 103–4.

27. See Seidler, "'Stifter einer weiteren Ahnenreihe?'" p. 76.

28. Becher, *Internationale Literatur*, June 1943, p. 5. See Fehervary, *Hölderlin and the Left*, p. 73.

29. See, for example, *Hölderlin. Heldentum. Auswahl für Soldaten*, ed. Amadeus Grohmann (Vienna and Leipzig: A. J. Walter, 1943).

30. Fehervary, *Hölderlin and the Left*, pp. 100–101. For another study of Hölderlin's reception among creative writers in postwar Germany, see Bernhard Greiner, "Zersprungene Identität. Bildnisse des Schriftstellers in zeitgenössischen Dichtungen über Hölderlin," in *Die deutsche Teilung im Spiegel der Literatur: Beiträge zur Literatur und Germanistik in der D.D.R.*, ed. Karl Lamers (Stuttgart: Bonn Aktuel, 1980), pp. 85–120; see also the above mentioned essays by Böschenstein and Seidler.

31. See Fehervary, *Hölderlin and the Left*, pp. 103–4.

32. Ibid., pp. 103–5.

33. Ibid., pp. 102–3, 110–15.

34. Stephan Hermlin, "Scardanelli," in *Sinn und Form* 3 (1970):513–34; Gerhard Wolf, *Der arme Hölderlin* (Berlin: Union Verlag, 1972). See Fehervary, *Hölderlin and the Left*, pp. 132–38, 142–53.

35. See Fehervary, *Hölderlin and the Left*, pp. 178–85.

36. See Seidler, "'Stifter einer weiteren Ahnenreihe?'" p. 81.

37. See Fehervary, *Hölderlin and the Left*, pp. 185–87.

38. Ibid., pp. 200–206.

39. Pierre Bertaux, *Hölderlin und die Französische Revolution* (Frankfurt am Main: Suhrkamp, 1969).

40. Peter Weiss, *Hölderlin* (Frankfurt am Main: Luchterhand, 1971). See Fehervary, *Hölderlin and the Left*, p. 206. For a discussion of the play, see Fehervary, pp. 206–14; Greiner, "Zersprungene Identität," pp. 100–103.

41. Peter Härtling, *Hölderlin: Ein Roman* (Darmstadt; Neuwied, 1976). For a brief discussion of the novel, see Greiner, "Zersprungene Identität," pp. 113–14.

42. Ryan, *Hölderlins Lehre vom Wechsel der Töne.*

43. Adolf Beck, "Hölderlin als Republikaner," *Hölderlin-Jahrbuch* 15 (1967–68):28–51.

44. See, for example, Gerhard Kurz, *Mittelbarkeit und Vereinigung; Zum Verhältnis von Poesie, Reflexion, und Revolution bei Hölderlin* (Stuttgart, 1975); and Johannes Mahr, *Mythos und Politik in Hölderlins Rheinhymne* (Munich, 1972).

45. See "Einleitung," pp. 16–17; see Fehervary, *Hölderlin and the Left,* pp. 234–38.

46. See the Bibliography for a listing of the volumes. For a benign appraisal of the entire project, see Gregor Thurmair, "Anmerkungen zur Frankfurter Hölderlin-Ausgabe," *Hölderlin-Jahrbuch* 22 (1980–81):371–89.

47. Bertaux, *Friedrich Hölderlin.*

48. See Adolf Beck, "Zu Pierre Bertauxs *Friedrich Hölderlin,*" in *Hölderlins Weg zu Deutschland: Fragments und Thesen* (Stuttgart, 1982), pp. 191–213.

49. See U. H. Peters, *Wider die These vom edlen Simulanten* (Reinbek bei Hamburg: Rowohlt, 1982).

Selected Bibliography

PRIMARY SOURCES

(It should be noted that the *Grosse Stuttgarter Ausgabe* is the standard edition and is used for all scholarly work on Hölderlin. The smaller editions of Lüders, Mieth, and [especially] Beissner/Schmidt all provide helpful interpretive notes. The *Frankfurter Ausgabe* is useful in that it offers transcriptions of Hölderlin's manuscripts.)

Hölderlin: Sämtliche Werke. Grosse Stuttgarter Ausgabe. Edited by Friedrich Beissner and Adolf Beck. 7 vols. Stuttgart: Cotta, 1943–1977.

Hölderlin: Werke und Briefe. Edited by Friedrich Beissner and Jöchen Schmidt. 2 vols. Frankfurt am Main: Insel, 1969.

Hölderlin, Friedrich. Sämtliche Werke und Briefe. Edited by Gunther Mieth. 2 vols. Munich: Carl Hansen, 1970.

Hölderlin, Friedrich. Sämtliche Gedichte. Edited by Detlev Lüders. Bad Homburg: Athenäum, 1970.

Hölderlin, Friedrich. Sämtliche Werke. Frankfurter Ausgabe. Edited by D. E. Sattler and W. Groddek. Frankfurt am Main: Roter Stern, 1975–. The following volumes have appeared:
"Einleitung" (1975)
Vol. 6: "Elegien und Epigramme" (1976)
Vol. 3: "Iambische und hexametrische Formen" (1977)
Vol. 2: "Lieder und Hymnen" (1978)
Vol. 14: "Entwürfe zur Poetik" (1979)
Vol. 10/11: *"Hyperion"* (1982)

1. Translations

Poems and Fragments. Translated by Michael Hamburger. Ann Arbor: University of Michigan, 1967. The most complete set of English translations of Hölderlin's poems.

Selected Poems by Friedrich Hölderlin and Eduard Mörike. Translated with an introduction by Christopher Middleton. Chicago: University of Chicago Press, 1972.

2. Bibliographies

Kohler, Maria, and Kelletat, Arthur. *Hölderlin-Bibliographie 1938-1950.* Publication of the Hölderlin-Archive. Stuttgart: Landesbibliothek, 1953.

Current bibliography, edited by Maria Kohler, has been appearing in issues of the *Hölderlin-Jahrbuch* since the 1955/56 issue. One should also consult the Hölderlin sections of the annual bibliographies published in *PMLA* and of the current bibliographies of the romantic movement published in *ELN* and earlier (1950–65) in *PQ*.

Seebass, Friedrich. *Hölderlin-Bibliographie*. Munich: H. Stobbe, 1922.

SECONDARY SOURCES

(In the following sections I have limited myself to listing book-length studies which, in my opinion, would most likely be of use to the beginning student of Hölderlin.)

1. Biographical Studies in Foreign Languages

Beck, Adolf, and Raabe, Paul. *Hölderlin: Eine Chronik in Text und Bild*. Frankfurt am Main: Insel, 1970. The most complete chronology of Hölderlin's life.

Beissner, Friedrich. *Reden und Aufsätze*. Weimar: Böhlau, 1961. Includes a number of biographical essays.

Bertaux, Pierre. *Hölderlin. Essai de biographie intérieure*. Paris: Hachette, 1936. Tentative analytical biography.

Kempter, Lothar. *Hölderlin in Hauptwil*. St. Gallen: Tschudy, 1946. An investigation of Hölderlin's brief stay with the Gonzenbach family.

Kirchner, Werner. *Hölderlin: Aufsätze zu seiner Homburger Zeit*. Göttingen: Vandenhoek & Ruprecht, 1967.

―――. *Der Hochverratprozess gegen Sinclair*. Marburg am Lahn: Simons, 1949. A detailed account of Sinclair's treason trial and its effect on Hölderlin.

Laplanche, Jean. *Hölderlin et la question du père*. Paris: Presses Universitaires de France, 1961. Translated as *Hölderlin und die Suche nach dem Vater* (Stuttgart-Bad Cannstadt: Frommann-Holzboog, 1975). An analysis of Hölderlin in terms of Lacanian psychology.

Michel, Wilhelm. *Das Leben Friedrich Hölderlins*. Bremen: Carl Schünemann; Frankfurt: Insel, 1967. The standard biography.

2. Critical Studies in Foreign Languages

Aspetsberger, Friedbert. *Welteinheit und epische Gestaltung: Hölderlins "Hyperion."* Munich: Wilhelm Fink, 1971.

Beck, Adolf. *Hölderlins Weg zu Deutschland: Fragmente und Thesen*. Stuttgart: Metzler, 1982. Beck and Beissner (see following two entries) were perhaps the foremost Hölderlin scholars of their time.

Beissner, Friedrich. *Hölderlin: Reden und Aufsätze*. See earlier entry.

―――. *Hölderlins Übersetzungen aus dem Griechischer*. 2d ed. Stuttgart: Metzler, 1961. An analysis of the Pindar and Sophocles translations.

Binder, Wolfgang. *Hölderlin-Studien.* Frankfurt am Main: Insel, 1970. A collection of interpretive essays by a distinguished critic.

Böckmann, Paul. *Hölderlin und seine Götter.* Munich: C. H. Beck, 1935. A monument of older Hölderlin scholarship.

Böschenstein, Bernhard. *Hölderlins Rheinhymne.* 2d ed. Zurich: Atlantis, 1968. A thorough interpretation of an important poem.

Gaier, Ulrich. *Der gesetzliche Kalkül: Hölderlins Dichtungslehre.* Tübingen: Niemeyer, 1962. An attempt to synthesize Hölderlin's theory of literature.

Gilby, William. *Das Bild des Feuers bei Hölderlin: Eine genetische Betrachtung.* Bonn: Bouvier, 1973. Study of an important symbolic motif in Hölderlin's poetry.

Häny, Arthur. *Hölderlins Titanenmythos.* Zurich: Atlantis, 1948. An attempt to interpret one of the more important fragmentary hymns.

Hof, Walter. *Hölderlins Stil als Ausdruck seiner geistigen Welt.* Meisenheim a. Glan: Anton Hain, 1956. An analysis of Hölderlin's style.

Hoffmeister, Johannes. *Hölderlin und die Philosophie.* 2d ed. Leipzig: F. Meiner, 1944. Studies Hölderlin's relationship to the thought of his time.

Hölscher, Uvo. *Empedokles und Hölderlin.* Frankfurt: Insel, 1965. A helpful introduction to Hölderlin's Empedokles dramas.

Hötzer, Ulrich. *Die Gestalt des Herakles in Hölderlins Dichtung.* Stuttgart: Kohlhammer, 1956. Study of an important motif.

Kempter, Lothar. *Hölderlin und die Mythologie.* Zurich and Leipzig: Horgen, 1929. A still valuable work of research.

Kudszus, Winfried. *Sprachverlust und Sinnwandel: Zur späten und spätesten Lyrik Hölderlins.* Stuttgart: Metzler, 1969. Interpretive essays on a number of Hölderlin's late poems and fragments.

Kurz, Gerhard. *Mittelbarkeit und Vereinigung: Zur Verhältnis von Poesie, Reflexion und Revolution bei Hölderlin.* Stuttgart: Metzler, 1975. Examines the relationship of Hölderlin's political ideals to his poetic theory and practice.

Mahr, Johannes. *Mythos und Politik in Hölderlins Rheinhymne.* Munich: Wilhelm Fink, 1972. As the title suggests, an analysis of the relationship between mythic and political thinking in "Der Rhein."

Mieth, Günther. *Friedrich Hölderlin.* East Berlin: Rütten & Loening, 1978. A general study of Hölderlin from a Marxist perspective.

Müller, Ernst. *Hölderlin: Studien zur Geschichte seines Geistes.* Stuttgart and Berlin: Kohlhammer, 1944. An analysis of the poet's intellectual and philosophical development.

Pellegrini, Alessandro. *Friedrich Hölderlin: Sein Bild in der Forschung.* Berlin: De Gruyter, 1965. A comprehensive study of the academic response to Hölderlin from the nineteenth century to ca. 1960.

Raabe, Paul. *Die Briefe Hölderlins; Studien zur Entwicklung und Persönlichkeit des Dichters.* Stuttgart: Metzler, 1963. Psychological analysis of Hölderlin's letters.

Ryan, Lawrence. *Friedrich Hölderlin.* 2d ed. Stuttgart: Metzler, 1967. The standard brief, scholarly introduction to the poet.

———. *Hölderlins Hyperion: Exzentrische Bahn und Dichterberuf.* Stuttgart: Metzler, 1965. Landmark analysis of the novel, to which all later criticism must refer.

———. *Hölderlins Lehre vom Wechsel der Töne.* Stuttgart: Kohlhammer, 1960. Ambitious attempt to elucidate the theoretical writings, and a major event in the history of Hölderlin criticism.

Schmidt, Jochen. *Hölderlins Elegie "Brod und Wein."* Berlin: De Gruyter, 1968. Thorough and comprehensive analysis of the poem.

———. *Hölderlins letzte Hymnen "Andenken" und "Mnemosyne."* Tübingen: Niemeyer, 1970. Detailed analyses of the poems.

———. *Hölderlins später Widerruf in den Oden "Chiron," "Blödigkeit" und "Ganymed."* Tübingen: Niemeyer, 1978. Detailed analyses of several of the later odes.

Schmidt, Jochen, ed. *Über Hölderlin.* Frankfurt am Main: Insel, 1970. An anthology of some of the more important twentieth-century essays on the poet.

Söring, Jürgen. *Die Dialektik der Rechtfertigung: Überlegungen zu Hölderlins Empedokles-Projekt.* Frankfurt am Main: Athenäum, 1973. Subtle and detailed analyses of the Empedokles dramas and related theoretical writings.

Stoll, Robert Thomas. *Hölderlins Christushymnen: Grundlegung und Darstellung.* Basel: Schwabe, 1952. Good, clearly written discussions of some of the later hymns.

Szondi, Peter. *Hölderlin-Studien. Mit einem Traktat über philologische Erkenntnis.* 2d ed. Frankfurt am Main: Insel, 1970. Stimulating analyses of some of Hölderlin's poems.

Viëtor, Karl. *Die Lyrik Hölderlins.* Frankfurt am Main: Moritz Diesterweg, 1921. Still useful formal analyses of Hölderlin's lyric poetry.

Walser, Jürg Peter. *Hölderlin Archipelagus.* Zurich: Atlantis, 1962. Thorough and comprehensive study of the poem.

Zuberbühler, Rolf. *Hölderlins Erneuerung der Sprache aus ihren etymologischen Ursprüngen.* Berlin: E. Schmidt, 1969. Interesting analysis of Hölderlin's use of language.

3. Critical Studies in English

Benn, M. B. *Hölderlin and Pindar.* 'S-Gravenhage: Mouton, 1962. Analyzes relationship between Hölderlin and the Greek poet.

Constantine, David J. *The Significance of Place in the Poetry of Friedrich Hölderlin.* London: Modern Humanities Research Association, 1979.

Fehervary, Helen. *Hölderlin and the Left: The Search for a Dialectic of Art and Life.* Heidelberg: Carl Winter, 1977. An interesting analytical survey of

Hölderlin's reception by the German left from the First World War to the present.

Gaskill, Peter H. "Christ and the Divine Economy in the Work of Friedrich Hölderlin." Ph. D. dissertation, Cambridge University, 1971. An analysis of the influence of German Pietism on Hölderlin, this study offers interesting insights into such poems as "Friedensfeier" and "Patmos."

George, Emery E., ed. *Friedrich Hölderlin: An Early Modern.* Ann Arbor: University of Michigan Press, 1972. A collection of interesting and often stimulating essays on the poet.

Harrison, R. B. *Hölderlin and Greek Literature.* Oxford: Clarendon Press, 1975.

Peacock, Ronald. *Hölderlin.* London: Methuen, 1938. A still useful general study of the poet.

Shelton, Roy C. *The Young Hölderlin.* Bern and Frankfurt am Main: Herbert Lang, 1973. A stimulating, if unsympathetic, psychological study of the poet's youth.

Silz, Walter. *Hölderlin's Hyperion: A Critical Reading.* Philadelphia: University of Pennsylvania Press, 1969. A helpful general study of the novel.

Unger, Richard. *Hölderlin's Major Poetry: The Dialectics of Unity.* Bloomington: University of Indiana Press, 1975. Offers detailed interpretations of some of Hölderlin's more important poems in terms of the poet's concern for the concept of All-Unity.

Index